WITHDRAWN

HIGH-TECH GRASS ROOTS

The Professionalization of Local Elections

J. CHERIE STRACHAN

ROWMAN & LITTLEFIELD PUBLISHERS, INC.
Lanham • Boulder • New York • Oxford

ROWMAN & LITTLEFIELD PUBLISHERS, INC.

Published in the United States of America
by Rowman & Littlefield Publishers, Inc.
A Member of the Rowman & Littlefield Publishing Group
4720 Boston Way, Lanham, Maryland 20706
www.rowmanlittlefield.com

P.O. Box 317, Oxford OX2 9RU, United Kingdom

Copyright © 2003 by Rowman & Littlefield Publishers, Inc.

All rights reserved. No part of this publication may be reproduced, stored in a
retrieval system, or transmitted in any form or by any means, electronic,
mechanical, photocopying, recording, or otherwise, without the prior permission
of the publisher.

British Library Cataloguing in Publication Information Available

Library of Congress Cataloging-in-Publication Data

Strachan, J. Cherie, 1970–
    High-tech grass roots : the professionalization of local elections / J.
Cherie Strachan.
        p. cm. — (Campaigning American style)
    Includes bibliographical references and index.
        ISBN 0-7425-1765-9 (cloth : alk. paper) — ISBN 0-7425-1766-7 (pbk. :
alk. paper)
        1. Local elections—United States. 2. Campaign management—United
    States. 3. Political campaigns—United States. I. Title. II. Series.
    JS305 .S77 2003
    324.7'0973—dc21   2002011384

Printed in the United States of America

∞ ™ The paper used in this publication meets the minimum requirements of
American National Standard for Information Sciences—Permanence of Paper for
Printed Library Materials, ANSI/NISO Z39.48-1992.

CONTENTS

ACKNOWLEDGMENTS

S EVERAL PEOPLE WHO MADE significant contributions to this research project deserve recognition. First and foremost, I could not have asked for a better dissertation chair than Anne Hildreth. From the start, she supported my topic and helped me to design the research tools needed to investigate it. Most important, she provided this constructive criticism without dampening my enthusiasm for the project. Meanwhile, Kathy Kendall broadened my horizons by introducing me to literature of political communication. This research project, not to mention my future endeavors, surely benefited from the resulting interdisciplinary approach. Joseph Zimmerman's knowledge of local government structure was also invaluable. Last but not least, Dan Shea provided the encouragement I needed to pursue publication. Both he and Jennifer Knerr provided helpful insights as I conducted additional research and made substantial revisions to the original project.

Undertaking this project would have been much more difficult without the support of my family. Thanks to my husband, Dwayne, who not only moved hours away from friends and family, but also dedicated an entire summer to stuffing questionnaires into envelopes, organizing reference materials at the library, and entering coded data. Thanks also to my parents, who found countless ways to show their support throughout my years in graduate school. I will always remember the time they came to visit and insisted on buying me a computer desk. My Dad stubbornly claimed, "I'm not quite sure what a dissertation is, but I know you can't write one on a card table." He was right. The desk helped immensely, but not as much as the sentiment motivating its purchase.

The Latest Trends in U.S. Political Campaigns

Changes at the Grass Roots

In a recent campaign for office in the United States, a candidate carefully crafted his campaign messages according to information gleaned from a professionally conducted public opinion poll. With the aid of a well-known media production firm headquartered in Alexandria, Virginia, a series of broadcast television advertisements was produced and aired to communicate the candidate's theme. Meanwhile, a radio advertisement and direct-mail pieces were used to target voters with more specific messages. In addition, a website design firm was hired to create and manage the candidate's Internet site. All of these activities were coordinated by a professional campaign manager who had previously worked on the 1996 Clinton-Gore campaign. Overall, this particular candidate spent about $409,000 on his successful reelection bid, with nearly one-quarter of his budget dedicated to the purchase of airtime for his television commercials.[1]

Most observers of political campaigns in the United States would not find the preceding account particularly interesting. The tactics described are not new to the electoral scene. After all, the use of sophisticated tactics and campaign consultants has become commonplace in many types of elections. Presidential, senatorial, gubernatorial, and other statewide candidates, as well as candidates for the U.S. House and other local government offices serving large electorates—such as mayors in America's largest cities—would not be perceived as serious candidates unless their campaigns incorporated most of these types of activities, which typically require assistance from campaign professionals.[2] As one scholar notes: "Today few serious candidates . . . head out into the trenches without the aid of campaign consultants."[3]

Running for Mayor in Albany, New York

However, those interested in America's political campaigns might be more engaged by the preceding account upon learning that it detailed the activities of the incumbent mayor of Albany, New York, in the city's 1997 Democratic primary election. Although Albany is the state capital, the city's population at last count was only 95,658. Moreover, circumstances limit the city's effective electorate to registered Democratic voters. Until recently, the municipal government was controlled by a strong Democratic machine. While the machine's power has declined, registered voters in the city are still overwhelmingly aligned with the Democratic Party. In Albany, competitive races occur in the Democratic primary, whereas the general election is merely a formality. In 1997, for example, only 4,013 voters registered with the Republican Party, compared to 44,652 registered Democrats.[4] For all practical purposes, the members of the electorate who will choose the city's municipal officials are limited to these 44,652 voters eligible to vote in the Democratic primary election. Turnout in the 1997 Democratic mayoral primary was only 44 percent, as just under 20,000 voters went to the polls. The incumbent, Jerry Jennings, won the prized Democratic nomination with 11,760 votes. Thus, the incumbent mayor of a midsized city in upstate New York spent approximately thirty-five dollars per vote received in the primary to unleash a full array of sophisticated campaign activities on a relatively small, local electorate. This interesting mayoral campaign reveals that, at least in some cases, even the most local races have adopted the trappings of consultant-centered campaigns. Moreover, this particular race is not an isolated event, but is representative of an increasing number of elections at the grassroots level. As one newspaper editorial notes, more and more political candidates at the local level "are hiring outside consultants to advise them on everything from shirt color to speaking techniques."[5] While this phenomenon may not have been expected, a review of American political campaigns across the past several decades reveals that it is part of a continuing trend in the professionalization of electoral efforts.

The Transformation of Political Campaigns

The most significant change in electoral politics since the 1950s has been the way candidates run for office, and this transformation of American campaigns has been well-documented in all but the most local arenas. From the mid-1800s through most of the twentieth century, the political parties were actively involved in campaigning. "Candidates were expected to contribute to their election effort—often a donation to party coffers was a precondition of their nomination—but the task of voter contact was left to party activists."[6] Although the party organizations may not have dominated all contested races, many did maintain a core of loyal activists who could be counted on to carry candidates' messages to the voters. Campaigns relied on grass-

roots activities, such as holding rallies, canvassing door-to-door, and distributing literature, that depended on the face-to-face interaction between party
or campaign activists and voters. This dependence on volunteers does not
mean that well-funded candidates did not turn to the cutting-edge communication technology of the day. For example, they used the printing press to
mass-produce posters and handbills, photography to present candidate
images, and trains to conduct whistle-stop tours. Though these types of activities were incorporated into campaigns, they supplemented the efforts of
party activists, rather than replaced them.[7]

Reform movements aimed at eliminating the nation's corrupt urban
machines contributed to the end of these party-centered campaigns. The
adoption of civil service requirements deprived parties of some of the material
incentives they used to maintain a core of loyal activists, while the direct primary denied them exclusive power over the nomination of their candidates
for office. As these changes were taking effect, a revolution in communication
technology was occurring that allowed candidates to interact with their constituents without relying on party assistance. Forsaking the volunteer-intense
campaign tactics of party organizations, candidates began using polls to learn
voter concerns and advertising through electronic media to communicate
directly with the electorate, and thus developed what came to be called "new-
style campaigning."[8]

Sophisticated campaigns for office first took root at the presidential level
in key states such as California. When candidates for national and statewide
office began winning, their tactics were quickly adopted by others. Some of
the first well-publicized sophisticated campaigns were Richard Nixon's 1948
efforts to win a Senate seat in California, Jacob Javits's 1948 campaign for a
U.S. House seat in New York, and Winthrop Rockefeller's 1966 attempt to
claim the governor's office in Arkansas. By 1971, "the flood of technologi-
cally-oriented campaigns became a deluge."[9] Even mayoral candidates in
America's largest cities, for example, had adopted the new style of campaigning. In his unsuccessful 1969 bid to become mayor of Los Angeles, Tom
Bradley used polling and direct mail, as well as radio and television advertisements. George Voinovich had more luck in Cleveland's 1979 mayoral race.
He hired two firms—one to conduct public opinion polling and another to
produce commercials—and defeated his incumbent opponent.[10]

Coincidentally, Democratic Party reforms of the presidential nominating
process by the 1970s had further stripped party leaders' influence in nominating candidates, and campaign finance reform had led to the rapid increase in
the number of political action committees. These committees provided candidates with the financial means to purchase sophisticated communication
technology. Since candidates could obtain the essential resource of money
from these committees, the limited assistance that the parties were capable of
providing was further devalued.[11] By this point, the "new-style" campaigns

were widespread, and the transformation of party-centered elections into candidate-centered elections was complete.[12] Yet campaigns were still evolving. As candidates turned away from the parties for campaign assistance, they turned to "image makers" or marketing professionals who had mastered the new communication technologies that candidates needed to use in their campaigns. By the 1990s, the use of political consultants had become so widespread—even among candidates for the U.S. House of Representatives—that some suggested that U.S. political campaigns were most aptly described as consultant-centered.[13]

Old-Style versus New-Style Campaigns

The key to identifying new-style campaigns is in the sophistication of the tactics used to communicate with voters. Sophisticated tactics, which require the use of communication technologies and are difficult to master, were rarely found in old-style campaigns. Rather, old-style campaigns were primarily characterized by communication in its most basic format. In this format, without the use of creative innovations or modern technology, communication requires two or more people to be in the same geographic space at the same time. Relying on this method to communicate with more than a few people is impossible without a human labor force willing to invest time. As a result, old-style campaigns were reliant on volunteers. The grassroots activities they employed, such as canvassing door-to-door or holding rallies, required the resource of volunteers' and candidates' time. Yet throughout recorded history, human ingenuity has devised ways to break the barriers of time and space that limited human interactions. One of the most primitive examples is the paintings our ancestors left on cave walls to relay their hunting stories. These paintings illustrate that the skills needed to use some communications innovations are fairly easy to master. Old-style campaigns also incorporated some communication innovations when available, but they were not difficult for candidates or their volunteers to use. Examples include the production of campaign literature or the purchase of newspaper advertisements, which relied on the innovation of the printing press. Thus a list of the types of tactics characterizing traditional campaigns would include canvassing and dropping literature door-to-door, giving speeches, displaying yard signs, and running newspaper ads. The mid- to late-twentieth century, however, saw a dramatic increase in both the sophistication and the number of inventions breaking the time and/or space barriers of communication. Radios, televisions, computers, and, most recently, the Internet provided candidates with more effective ways of communicating across time and space. One of the primary differences between these innovations and those used in traditional campaigns is the difficulty of mastering the skills needed to use them. Talented volunteers can learn to draft newspaper copy, but few would be able to produce radio or television advertisements comparable in quality to those produced by professionals. Even fewer could master the intricacies of public opinion polling. Thus the resources needed to use the sophisticated tactics of new-style campaigns shifted away from time and toward the generalized resource of money, which could be used to purchase the new communications innovations, as well as the professional assistance needed to use them effectively. A list of the type of tactics characterizing new-style campaigns would include public opinion polls, television ads, targeted direct mail (which uses computer databases and mail-merge functions to identify likely voters), and radio ads, because such activities are undertaken most effectively with the assistance of campaign professionals.[14]

While both traditional and new-style tactics are used to relay persuasive messages to the electorate, traditional tactics rely on the resource of candidates' or volunteers' time, whereas the sophisticated tactics associated with new-style campaigns rely on the resource of money, which is needed to purchase both technology and expertise. It is important to note that these two types of tactics are not mutually exclusive; candidates can incorporate a mixture of both types in their efforts to communicate with voters throughout the duration of a political campaign. Yet any campaign relying heavily on sophisticated tactics—even if grassroots activities are not abandoned—is more accurately described as a new-style campaign because efforts to supplement traditional tactics have been made.

Changes in Smaller Electoral Districts

Descriptions of American candidates' adoption of new-style campaign strategies have been primarily limited to the activities of candidates with national or statewide constituencies, as well as to congressional candidates or those serving large local electorates. Some people contradicted conventional wisdom, claiming that sophistication would find its way into grassroots politics. In the late 1980s, for example, one observer pointed out that consultants had penetrated the "political boondocks," otherwise known as small towns in upstate New York.[15] At the same time, another argued that consulting would spread all the way down the ballot, with "the use of consultants, as well as the perception of the need for and dependency on them," continuing to grow.[16] In addition, while a comprehensive account of campaigns in small or midsized electoral districts has not been previously attempted, academic and journalistic accounts suggest that sophisticated tactics have been used in some small-constituency races.[17] Although the actual number of local government candidates across the nation using such tactics remains unknown, the executive director of the Center for Responsive Politics recently claimed, "Whatever office, whatever level of government, candidates are spending serious money on campaigns. And it winds up going to these consultants."[18]

Such accounts of new-style campaigns in local political arenas warrant a systematic investigation of the topic, especially when one considers the crucial role of elections in the maintenance of representative democracy. Yet the phenomenon has been heretofore largely overlooked.[19] One recent description of the consulting field, for example, indicates that the trend toward professionalization extends only to cities with a population of about 250,000. The practice is discounted in smaller elections—including those in towns, rural counties, and far down the ballot in big cities—with the claim that "these campaigns essentially count on name recognition and face-to-face meetings with voters, have low-budget advertising through posters, yard signs and last-minute advertisements in local newspapers."[20]

Perhaps observers of political campaigns want to cling to the romantic notion that at least one political arena in the United States will remain "pure" and unaffected by consultants' influences. Newspaper editorials, for example, often extol the virtues of local politicians who "tell it straight from their Bic pen to you, without the filter of a consultant."[21] A more plausible reason, however, for the lack of studies on new-style campaigns at the local level has been the assumption that candidates who need to reach comparatively small numbers of voters can do so effectively via traditional grassroots activities. Both scholars and practitioners have included a large constituency as one of the conditions that must exist before candidates will hire political consultants to work on their campaigns.[22] Consultants' assistance in competitive national and state government races is expected, as "candidates running for offices with large constituencies simply cannot communicate effectively to a sufficient number of voters without using communication technology and consultants with the expertise to employ those technologies effectively."[23] On the other hand, "candidates running for small constituency offices are likely to feel that they can personally contact enough of the voters to win on their own, without any help or with exceedingly limited help."[24] This conventional wisdom has been persuasive because it is based on logical assumptions about the costs and benefits of using sophisticated tactics. Why bother with the expense and complexity of new-style campaign tactics if these are not essential to communicating with the electorate? Although the reasons behind these candidates' adoption of sophisticated tactics remain unclear, both advances in communication technology and changes in the political consulting field can account for the feasibility—if not the adoption—of new-style campaigns in local electoral arenas.

The Feasibility of Local Sophistication

The assumption that local candidates would continue to run traditional campaigns held true when the sophisticated tactics of new-style campaigns were first available to candidates. The technology was best suited to broadcasting the same campaign messages to large numbers of people, and it was prohibitively expensive. Moreover, the professional assistance required to incorporate sophisticated tactics was not readily available at the grassroots level. As the groundbreaking study on the consulting field accurately notes, researching the profession at the time involved examining "the relatively small and elite corps of interstate political consultants who usually work on many campaigns simultaneously and have served hundreds of campaigns in their careers."[25] Conventional wisdom based on these descriptive accounts overlooks further technological advancements and changes in the field of political consulting that make new-style campaign strategies a feasible option for local candidates.

Improvements in production processes resulted in the decreased cost of communication technology. For example, the price of television sets and home computers plummeted. While more affordable communication technology brought sophisticated tactics into local candidates' price ranges, it also enabled more people to enter the profession of political consulting. Access to computers is a prerequisite for many consulting specialties. The decreased cost of computers reduced the start-up expenses for opening a consulting business, resulting in these firms springing up in regions of the country other than Washington, D.C., or California. Membership in the American Association of Political Consultants rose from merely 50 to over 3,500 members.[26] This shift in the consulting field was also revealed by a 1990 survey conducted by the *National Journal,* indicating that the industry was splintering into more numerous, smaller firms.[27] In order to turn a profit and to build a track record, these firms are more willing to take on candidates who would be viewed as undesirable by larger, more prestigious firms. Although an elite corps of prominent political consultants who work on high-visibility races still exists, a larger pool of skilled professionals has developed.

Finally, further technological development made it possible to use sophisticated tactics to communicate with smaller groups of people. Advances such as cable television and computerized mail merges allowed local government candidates to communicate with voters in their own electoral districts, rather than with those in a larger broadcast media market. As communication consultants would say, the most recent technology provides the ability to "narrowcast," rather than to broadcast, messages. Decreases in computer prices and user-friendly software packages designed for campaigns have even made the sophisticated tactic of identifying specific demographic groups within electoral districts a possibility for local campaigns. These trends led state legislative candidates to adopt the trappings of new-style campaigns by the early 1980s.[28] There is no reason to believe that these trends have not continued since the 1980s, making new-style campaigns a feasible alternative in ever-smaller political units.[29]

Although these developments help to explain how sophisticated campaigns in smaller electoral districts became feasible, they do not explain why local candidates decided to expend the additional effort needed to adopt such tactics. The apparent irrationality of such decisions is further illuminated by understanding the factors that typically affect the adoption of technological innovations.[30] One of the best predictors of whether an innovation will be adopted is the perceived relative advantage it provides over the idea it supersedes.[31] "There are a number of subdimensions of relative advantage: the degree of economic profitability, low initial cost, a decrease in discomfort, savings in time and effort, and the immediacy of the reward."[32] In this case, local government candidates would consider using sophisticated tactics when lower initial cost and the improved ability to target desired voters enhanced their perceptions of the relative advantages that such tactics could provide.

Yet before sophisticated tactics are actually adopted, local government candidates must believe that these provide an advantage over grassroots activities and must perceive that using new-style campaign tactics to supplement or replace traditional tactics will be an improvement. At this point, the persuasiveness of the conventional wisdom about local campaigns becomes apparent. For while campaign tactics requiring direct, personal contact are a time-consuming, inefficient way to reach large numbers of voters, they are also the most persuasive weapons in a campaigner's arsenal. "Simply put, there is no better way of winning a vote than to have the candidate ask for it."[33] Hence, candidates running in large electorates turn to sophisticated tactics out of necessity. In an era when candidates cannot rely on a core of faithful party volunteers to carry their messages directly to voters, they need communication technology to reach their electorate. For candidates in national and statewide races, communication technology is a necessity, rather than a luxury. Candidates running for small-constituency offices are capable of making persuasive, direct contact with voters. Even if the relative advantage of using sophisticated tactics has improved, these are not a necessity in smaller local political arenas. More important, they are less effective at achieving a candidate's ultimate goal of persuasion.

Mayor Jennings Contradicts Conventional Wisdom

A return to the example of Albany's 1997 mayoral election, however, reveals that candidates in local government races are turning to such tactics despite their ability to achieve direct contact with most voters. According to his campaign manager, the incumbent Jerry Jennings canvassed the entire city, including the households of all registered Democratic or Republican voters.[34] (This was unusual since Republicans could not vote in the primary election. Given the small number of Republicans in Albany, however, it probably did not require much additional effort to include them in canvassing efforts.)

Even if his manager's claims exaggerated the number of people contacted, descriptions of Jennings's campaign tactics in the local newspaper indicated a strong grassroots effort. As the primary election date approached, an article reported that Jennings planned to walk the streets for three to four hours and visit several neighborhood block parties.[35] When asked about these grassroots activities, he said, "We don't want people to be apathetic. That's why I'm continuing to keep this pace."[36] Another account described him visiting soccer camps, black churches, and senior citizen housing, as well as working up a sweat by "jogging through neighborhoods, ringing doorbells, and shaking hands."[37] Even the public opinion poll commissioned by the Albany newspaper, the *Times Union,* indicated that Jennings was "pounding the pavement." Responses to the poll found that the mayor had personally contacted twice as many people as his opponent had.[38] Furthermore, "of those who had received a visit from only one candidate, three times as many said it was Jennings who showed up at their door."[39]

Despite this ability to reach out directly to voters, Jennings also relied on sophisticated tactics and prominent political consultants to win his bid for re-election. While Jennings spent his time during the campaign personally contacting scores of voters, pollsters gauged reaction to his campaign with public opinion polls, and media consultants reinforced his campaign theme with broadcast television advertisements. Even though his grassroots effort superseded that of his opponent, Jennings still felt the need to incorporate an additional layer of sophisticated tactics and professional services. When questioned about his reasons for doing so, Jennings simply said, "We're doing what we have to do."[40] Comparing the 1997 race to the previous mayoral election, Jennings suggested that the sophisticated tactics were intended to compensate for less press interest in the re-election bid, as well as limits on his ability to campaign in person. (In 1993, he had been an assistant high school principal, with free time during the summer months for campaigning.)[41] For unknown reasons, Jennings believed that his substantial grassroots efforts alone could not guarantee his re-election, so he decided to adopt the tactics of new-style campaigning.

Sophisticated Campaigning Takes Root in Southlake, Texas, and Dunedin, Florida

Other local candidates, from states spread across the country, have apparently reached similar conclusions. In 1998, Veronica "Ronnie" Kendall raised $18,150 to challenge an incumbent city council member in Southlake, Texas, population 21,519.[42] Kendall relied on her own campaign experience, gained from working on her husband's county-wide judicial races, to design direct-mail pieces targeted at specific constituents.[43] During her race, Kendall justified her campaign war chest, which was described as "staggering for a municipal election" with the statement: "Now we're entering the big time as a city. . . . You need more money to get the message out."[44] She pointed out that after her successful race, other Southlake candidates were quick to imitate her efforts.[45] The city's 2000 mayoral race is a recent example. Four-year incumbent Rick Stacey was opposed by another successful local politician, Debra Edmondson. Edmondson, who had been successful in all of her political endeavors since 1994, raised only $12,000 and spent months canvassing door-to-door. She lost the mayoral race with 1,696 of the 4,473 votes cast, after Stacey spent nearly $32,000, some of which was used to mail a promotional videotape to about half of the 6,900 homes in Southlake.[46]

Another local candidate, Deborah Kynes, initiated a similar trend in Dunedin, Florida, population 35,691. In 1999, Kynes, a Clearwater lawyer, was one of four candidates vying for two open seats on the Dunedin City Commission. She raised $13,000 and hired a local political consulting firm, Repper, Garcia, and Associates. As a result, she captured by far the most votes—3,219 of 4,658 ballots cast—and won in every precinct except one.[47] The other successful candidate in 1999 was Cecil Englebert, who had served on the city's commission seventeen years beforehand. He expressed surprise at the amount of money needed "just to keep up." "I did a lot of things . . . I'd never done before and spent more time advertising," he said.[48]

Candidates in the city's 2000 elections followed Kyne's example of sophisticated campaigning, leading local news reports to claim that "there's little doubt that politics in Dunedin are beginning to mirror what is happening in larger political arenas."[49] The incumbent mayor was re-elected without a challenge, but not before building a war chest of $16,000.[50] Meanwhile, four candidates, this time including two challengers and two incumbents, competed against each other to fill two seats on the city commission. Both incumbents, John Doglione and Janet Henderson, managed to retain their seats, but not without adjusting their campaign strategies.[51] Doglione, who had served four prior terms, described campaigning in Dunedin as becoming more difficult. While his past campaigns had been run with less than $3,000, he said, "It's a different story today. It's keeping up with the Joneses."[52] His comment may have been a reference to Henderson, who raised $11,000, of which $2,000 was spent to hire the same consulting firm used by Kynes. Her consultant, Wayne Garcia, described Dunedin's recent political campaigns as part of a national trend. "More people [local candidates] want to make sure they are prepared to get their message across. They are using more sophisticated means to get their message across," he said.[53]

Why Study Professionalization at the Grass Roots?

Despite the apparent logic of conventional wisdom about sophisticated campaign tactics, these two races provide anecdotal evidence of professionalization at the local level. Though local candidates have the ability to blanket their communities with persuasive face-to-face tactics, they are turning to the communication technology and professional expertise once reserved for high-visibility races. These two examples from consultant Wayne Garcia's clients, however, cannot reveal the breadth or the nature of this latest trend in American political campaigns. The extent and implications of the trend deserve further exploration because of the critical role that local elections play in maintaining American democracy. U.S. governments have democratic legitimacy because elections provide citizens with the opportunity to hold elected officials accountable. Elected officials gain the authority to make decisions on behalf of the public only after receiving approval from the electorate. According to Alexis de Tocqueville, the frequency of American elections in the 1800s ensured popular sovereignty. After describing the voters' role in choosing their lawgivers and executive agents, he wrote, "The people reign over the American political world as God rules over the universe."[54]

Since elections are the primary mechanisms enabling popular sovereignty, any changes in their structure or context that might affect citizens' ability to effectively participate in electoral politics deserve to be examined. Note that whether or not members of the electorate utilize their abilities to influence local elections is a separate, although equally important, question. Even when opportunities for political influence exist, some people may not take advantage of them, particularly in traditionalist political cultures where elite control is expected.[55] Structuring electoral politics to optimize citizens' opportunities for influence does not guarantee people's participation. Yet it is an essential prerequisite for democratic rule. As such, the structure of electoral politics is worthy of scholarly attention.

Indeed, research has addressed the rise of new-style campaigning in elections with larger electorates. In addition to providing descriptive accounts, studies have also addressed whether new-style campaigns hinder the public's use of elections as a mechanism of accountability. Topics of research include, but are not limited to, whether political consultants—or unaccountable "hired guns"—have undue influence in the electoral process; whether communication technology provides candidates with an unprecedented ability to make deceptive, emotion-laden, or negative appeals; and whether candidates' need for money to purchase the trappings of new-style campaigns provides wealthy special interests with influence at the expense of average voters. As a result, some might suggest that resources need not be expended to examine new-style campaigns in local political arenas. One could argue that it is easier to study the campaigns of two presidential candidates or even one hundred gubernatorial candidates than to account for the campaigns of the significantly larger number of local government candidates in the United States. Thus, one could study electoral trends and their implications in national and state political races and expect those same implications to occur in local government arenas if candidates there adopt similar campaign strategies. Yet this latest development in the trend toward new-style campaigns deserves to be studied for a number of compelling reasons.

First, one should not underestimate the classic argument of federalism scholars that state and local political decisions are no less important than those made by public officials in Washington, D.C. Some even insist on describing the federal system as a noncentralized matrix, rather than as levels, to avoid the implication that states and local governing bodies are part of a hierarchy with the national government at the top.[56] Most elected officials in the United States serve in local governments. Although their individual actions affect smaller political units than the nation as a whole, when considered altogether their decisions have a major impact, especially in an era of increasing state and local government responsibilities. Consequently, changes in the dynamics of local electoral politics and the resulting effects on local political polities need to be explained simply because local politics are important.

Second, local politics does not occur in a vacuum. Events occurring in American communities have consequences for state and national politics. One particular concern associated with the adoption of local new-style campaigns is that the increased financial burdens could prevent candidates with lower socioeconomic status from running for office. Yet holding local elected positions often serves as a stepping-stone for politicians who pursue higher offices. Excluding an entire class of candidates from local races could further widen the socioeconomic gap between the electorate and their public officials and could affect the representativeness of all U.S. governing institutions. In addition, people learn how to participate in governing through the face-to-face interactions that occur in local political life. The roles they learn how to play are extended into state and national political activity. Thus, the increasing sophistication at the local level needs to be understood because of its far-reaching effects on the health of American democracy.

Third, the introduction of technology might not have an identical impact on local electoral politics as it does on state and national elections. Factors such as weak partisan identification and weak party influence on electoral outcomes compounded the impact of communication technology on national and state political campaigns. These factors may vary in different local governments. Local candidates also may have less access to financial resources other than the parties, which, if the case, would strengthen party influence on electoral politics. On the other hand, the widespread adoption of nonpartisan elections in small-constituency electoral districts may counteract any opportunities for partisan influence and may otherwise affect candidates' campaign choices. Local governments have a number of unique characteristics and responsibilities that could affect the dynamics of electoral politics. People also have different expectations for local government candidates and may notice if sophisticated tactics replace direct contact with voters. If such direct contact is sacrificed as a result of professionalization, an important opportunity to involve people in the governing process will be lost.

Finally, candidate-initiated communication is a more crucial element of the electorate's ability to hold public officials accountable at the local level. Campaign rhetoric is a less important resource for voters in larger electoral arenas because details about candidate character and issues are available from a wide variety of media sources.[57] Yet this type of rich information environment is less likely to exist in local government races. "One of the greatest ironies of the political process is that the higher the level of office sought, the greater amount of press scrutiny on the candidates."[58] In poor information environments—where candidates do not receive extensive coverage by the media—voters often base their perceptions on candidate advertisements.[59] This consequence is exacerbated in local political arenas, where rich information environments during campaigns for public office are often the exception, rather than the rule.

Gathering Information about Local Campaigns

For these reasons, this research represents an initial effort to address the existing gap in knowledge about American political campaigns. To adequately assess the role of new-style campaigns in local politics, three questions must be answered. They are: (1) How are local candidates running their campaigns for office? (2) What factors encourage their adoption of new-style campaign styles? and (3) How will their decisions affect local electoral politics? Providing adequate responses to each of these equally important questions required the development of multiple methodological approaches. To develop a descriptive account of local candidates' campaigns, as well as to explore whether consultants have promoted the adoption of sophisticated local campaigns, a mail survey of 607 general political consultants in the United states was conducted. The response rate was slightly more than 30 percent, with 185 consultants taking part. (For further details about the way the mail survey was conducted, see appendix A.)

The mail survey provides broad insight into the types of local government candidates who are turning to professional campaign assistance. Yet the local clientele of political consultants is not representative of all local candidates.

The fact that these clients hired consultants suggests that their campaigns were probably more sophisticated than those of candidates who did not feel the need for such assistance. Estimates of how widespread new-style campaigns are in local political arenas cannot be based on the mail survey alone. In addition, the mail survey was not designed to provide information about personal characteristics or the political environment that possibly affected candidates' strategic decisions. To gather such information and to gauge the extent of local candidates' adoption of new-style campaigns, telephone interviews with an average length of fifteen minutes were conducted with local political reporters in midsized cities with a mayor-council form of government. (Midsized cities were defined as those with a population ranging from 50,000 to 250,000 residents.) The difficulty posed by the sheer number of elected officials in the United States affected this choice. The decision was made to develop an account of a particular subset of local candidates—mayoral candidates in midsized cities—rather than a descriptive account of all local candidates' campaigns. A total of 142 cities had both an appropriate population size and a mayor-council form of government.[60] This research design focuses on cities meeting these two criteria, instead of on the equal representation of states or regions of the country. Similarly, no effort was made to balance the number of cities falling within specific population categories. Since smaller cities are more numerous than larger ones across the United States, they make up a larger percentage of the cities studied. As indicated by table 1.1, a majority of the cities—53 percent—has 79,999 or fewer residents. Telephone interviews were completed in 109 of these 142 cities, producing a response rate of nearly 77 percent. Altogether, information was collected about the campaigns of 217 candidates who ran in these 109 cities' most recent mayoral elections. Some of these candidates were unopposed, while others ran in two-candidate and multiple-candidate races. In the latter, reporters were asked to exclude information about fringe candidates who made little or no campaigning efforts. (For more details about the way the telephone interviews were conducted, see appendix A.)

When combined, the mail survey and telephone interviews provide insight into local candidates' reliance on political consultants, as well as on the adoption of new-style campaigns by a particular subset of local candidates. Yet neither provides in-depth understanding of local campaigns in a specific city. Accounts of competitive mayoral races in Albany, New York's Democratic primary elections were gathered to provide this type of qualitative insight. The number of competitive races in Albany has been limited by the control of a Democratic machine. Despite this, the city's longtime machine incumbent, Mayor Erastus Corning, faced serious challenges in 1973 and 1977. Since then, machine control has diminished, resulting in more competitive races for the Democratic nomination. In 1993, a Democratic councilman and the chair of the local Democratic Party competed

Table 1.1 The Prevalence of Smaller Cities with Mayors in the United States

Population	Frequency	Population	Frequency
50,000–59,999	33	150,000–159,999	2
60,000–69,999	25	160,000–169,999	2
70,000–79,999	17	170,000–179,999	3
80,000–89,999	16	180,000–189,999	3
90,000–99,999	4	190,000–199,999	5
100,000–109,999	10	200,000–209,999	2
110,000–119,999	4	210,000–219,999	0
120,000–129,999	3	220,000–229,999	4
130,000–139,999	3	230,000–239,999	1
140,000–149,999	4	240,000–250,000	1

$N = 142$, which includes all the U.S. cities with both a mayor/council form of government and a population falling between 50,000 and 250,000 residents.

Sources: U.S. Bureau of the Census. 1994. *County and City Databook* (Washington, D.C.: U.S. Government Printing Office, 1994); and *The Municipal Yearbook, 1996* (Washington, D.C.: International City/County Management Association, 1996).

against each other for an open mayoral seat. The winner of that race, former councilman Jerry Jennings, was challenged by a Democratic state assemblyman in 1997. Details and examples of campaign rhetoric were gathered from newspaper accounts in the Albany newspaper, the *Times Union,* and from personal interviews with candidates and their campaign staff. All candidates and members of their campaign staffs were interviewed, with the exception of Corning, who is deceased, and Jennings, who is the current incumbent.

Finally, to extend the qualitative insight provided by the Albany case study beyond the Northeast, vignettes of sophisticated local campaigns in other areas of the country were developed. Races where candidates hired consultants or relied on sophisticated communication technology were identified via regional newspaper databases. These newspaper accounts were supplemented with personal interviews. Particular races were selected for inclusion not only to provide accounts of recent campaign activities at the local level, but also to reflect the diversity in regions of the country where professionalization is taking root and in the types of local candidates who are incorporating sophisticated tactics.

Overview of the Book

The data collected through these efforts will be used to answer the three questions posed earlier. Chapters 2 through 4 detail empirical findings. Chapter 2 provides a descriptive account of campaigns in U.S. midsized electoral districts, which indicates that substantial numbers of candidates in these districts have added a layer of sophisticated tactics to their campaigns. Chapter 3 explores factors associated with these candidates' decisions to adopt new-style campaigns. Since the factors that promote sophistication, such as competitive races, contact with professional consultants, and shifting expectations about campaign styles, will continue to affect candidates' choices, the chapter concludes that the trend toward local campaign sophistication is both progressive and irreversible. Chapter 4 provides an analysis of how local campaign processes are being affected by these candidates' campaign choices. It notes that since local candidates have not abandoned traditional grassroots tactics, the benefits provided by face-to-face interaction between candidates and citizens have been preserved. Hence, shifting toward new-style campaigns increases the available amount of information about local politics and reaches beyond the core of active voters typically contacted in grassroots efforts. Yet findings reveal that this potential benefit is offset by several negative consequences; for example, the shift toward new-style campaigns discourages those from lower socioeconomic backgrounds from running for office, exacerbates the importance of raising funds from monied interests, and allows inequities in campaign budgets to affect the type of information that is available to voters. Chapter 5 responds to such concerns by exploring potential reforms to improve citizens' abilities to hold their public officials accountable in an era of encroaching new-style local campaigns. In particular, it argues that changes will need to focus on preventing the appearance of undue influence and on supporting challengers to ensure socioeconomic diversity among those serving as public officers. Reformers, however, will need to be creative in responding to these concerns in local government, as some of the most obvious solutions are not feasible.

Notes

1. Jay Jochnowitz, "A Shift in the Political Sand," *Times Union* (Albany, N.Y.), 7 September 1997, 1(A); Jay Jochnowitz, "Jennings, McEneny Duel with Ads," *Times Union* (Albany, N.Y.), 1 September 1997, 1(B); Jay Jochnowitz, "Campaign Costs Up Stakes for Candidates," *Times Union* (Albany, N.Y.), 15 March 1998, 1(D); and Karen Persichilli, Jennings campaign manager, telephone interview by J. Cherie Strachan. Tape recording, May 1998.

2. In summarizing the results of six case studies of recent, competitive House races, for example, Thurber concludes that "those who win congressional campaigns, by chance or by necessity, have highly professional organizations, retaining general strategists, pollsters, media consultants field (or get-out-the-vote) organizers, opposition research experts and fund raisers." James A. Thurber, "Introduction," in *The Battle for Congress, Consultants, Candidates and Voters,* ed. James A. Thurber (Washington, D.C.: Brookings Institution Press, 2001), 4.

3. Daniel M. Shea, *Campaign Craft: The Strategies, Tactics and Art of Political Campaign Management* (Westport, Conn.: Praeger, 1996), 13.

4. Jay Jochnowitz, "Viewing November Elections through GOP-Colored Glasses," *Times Union* (Albany, N.Y.), 14 October 1997, 5(B).

5. Nancy Johnson, "Running for Office Can Be an Education," *South Bend Tribune*, 30 April 2000, 1(F).

6. Shea, *Campaign Craft*, 7.

7. Early technology also gave political candidates greater control over the content of their campaign rhetoric. According to McGerr, the advertising style of campaign rhetoric often associated with modern political campaigns was well-established by the 1920s. Yet the technology of the day did not enable candidates to avoid party assistance for the delivery of these campaign messages. See Michael McGerr, *The Decline of Popular Politics: The American North, 1865–1928* (New York: Oxford Press, 1986).

8. Robert Agranoff, *The New Style in Election Campaigns* (Boston: Holbrook, 1972).

9. Benjamin Ginsberg, *The Captive Public* (New York: Basic, 1986), 165.

10. Jerry Hagstrom and Robert Guskind, "Mayoral Candidates Enter the Big Time Using Costly TV Ads and Consultants," *National Journal* (6 April 1985): 737.

11. Shea, *Campaign Craft*, 7.

12. For a more detailed account of the shift from party-centered to candidate-centered campaigns, see Martin Wattenberg, *The Rise of Candidate-Centered Politics: Presidential Elections of the 1980s* (Cambridge: Harvard University Press, 1991); and Barbara G. Salamore and Stephen A. Salamore, *Candidates, Parties and Campaigns: Electoral Politics in America*, 2nd ed. (Washington D.C.: CQ Press, 1989).

13. Shea, *Campaign Craft*, 13.

14. Herrnson identifies the same types of tactics as more complex, noting that polling and advertising are "highly technical campaign activities that require the involvement of individuals with specialized skill," and that "some media such as television, radio and direct mail, require the services of highly specialized personnel." Paul Herrnson, "Hired Guns and House Races: Campaign Professionals in House Races" in *Campaign Warriors: The Role of Political Consultants in Elections*, ed. James A. Thurber and Candice J. Nelson (Washington, D.C.: Brookings Institution Press, 2000), 73 and 81.

15. Benjamin Ginsberg, "A Post-Electoral Era?" *PS: Political Science* 22, no. 1 (March 1989): 18.

16. Walter DeVries, "American Campaign Consulting: Trends and Concerns," *PS: Political Science* 22, no. 1 (March 1989): 22.

17. Johnson suggests that such activities began in the mid-1990s and that hundreds of candidates below the statewide and congressional level have now hired professional assistance on their campaigns. Dennis Johnson, "The Business of Political Consulting," in *Campaign Warriors: The Role of Political Consultants in Elections*, ed. James A. Thurber and Candice J. Nelson (Washington, D.C.: Brookings Institution Press, 2000), 24. Also see Hagstrom and Guskind, "May-

oral Candidates Enter the Big Time," 737; Clea Benson and John Borland, "Professional Campaign Help Goes Local," *California Journal* (November 1994): 13–17; and Rita Kirk Whillock, *Political Empiricism: Communication Strategies in State and Regional Elections* (New York: Praeger, 1991).

18. As quoted by Leslie Wayne, "Political Consultants Thrive in the Cash-Rich New Politics," *New York Times,* 24 October 2000, 28(A).

19. Much of the research on consultants explores the role they play in more prominent up-ballot races. A recent survey of U.S. consultants, for example, restricted the sample to those consultants working in firms associated with presidential, Senate, or congressional campaigns in at least one of the past three election cycles. James A. Thurber, Candice J. Nelson, and David A. Dulio, "Portrait of Campaign Consultants," in *Campaign Warriors: The Role of Political Consultants in Elections,* ed. James A. Thurber and Candice J. Nelson (Washington, D.C.: Brookings Institution Press, 2000), 10–36.

20. Dennis W. Johnson, *No Place for Amateurs* (New York: Routledge, 2001), xv.

21. Bill Bishop, "Truth in Advertising," *Herald-Leader* (Lexington, Ky.), 6 May 1998, 15(A).

22. Robert V. Friedenberg, *Communication Consultants in Political Campaigns* (Westport, Conn.: Praeger, 1997), 5. The other three preconditions he describes are evenly contested races, aggressive candidates, and sufficient funds or volunteers.

23. Friedenberg, *Communication Consultants,* 5.

24. Friedenberg, *Communication Consultants,* 5. Friedenberg does not provide a more precise definition of large- and small-constituency districts. However, the definition of a small constituency seems to be based on a candidate's ability to reach a substantial percentage of the registered voters within the district through traditional grassroots activities.

25. Larry Sabato, *The Rise of Political Consultants* (New York: Basic, 1981), 8.

26. Shea, *Campaign Craft,* 13.

27. Jerry Hagstrom, "Spreading the Load," *National Journal* (20 October 1990): 2529–31.

28. Salamore and Salamore, *Candidates, Parties and Campaigns,* 220–23.

29. For an account of local candidates' use of cable, see James M. Hoefler, "Cable Television Advertising and Subnational Elections," *Comparative State Politics* (April 1990): 37–42; and Robert Guskind, "Cable Connection," *National Journal* (19 September 1992): 2111. For an account of their use of Internet sites, see Graeme Browning, "Medium Cool," *National Journal* (19 October 1996): 2223.

30. Everett M. Rogers, *Diffusion of Innovations,* 3rd ed. (New York: Free Press, 1983), 38–85.

31. Rogers, *Diffusion of Innovations,* 213–17.

32. Rogers, *Diffusion of Innovations,* 218.

33. Shea, *Campaign Craft,* 241.

34. Persichilli interview.

35. Tim O'Brien, "Their Final Goal Is a Win Tuesday," *Times Union* (Albany, N.Y.), 7 September 1997, 1(D).

36. O'Brien, "Their Final Goal," 1(D).

37. Bechetta Jackson, "Shoe-Leather Time in Mayoral Race," *Times Union* (Albany, N.Y.), 8 September 1997, 1(A).

38. Jay Jochnowitz and Tim O'Brien, "Poll Gives Jennings Big Lead," *Times Union* (Albany, N.Y.), 31 August 1997, 1(A).

39. Jochnowitz and O'Brien, 6(A). The poll, conducted by Zogby International, was based on interviews with 406 likely Democratic primary voters and had a margin of error of + or − 5.

40. Jay Jochnowitz, "A Shift in the Political Sand," *Times Union* (Albany, N.Y.), 7 September 1997, 3(A).

41. Jochnowitz, "A Shift in the Political Sand," 1(A) and 3(A).

42. This amount was obtained from campaign finance reports filed with the Texas Ethics Commission.

43. Veronica Kendall telephone interview, by J. Cherie Strachan. Tape recording, September 2001.

44. Marisa Taylor, "Southlake Candidate Raises the Bar in Financing Race," *Fort Worth Star-Telegram*, 8 April 1998, 6.

45. Kendall interview.

46. Mike Lee, "Candidate Reflects on Loss in Race for Mayor," *Fort-Worth Star Telegram*, 12 May 2000, 1; and Mike Lee, *Fort-Worth Telegraph* reporter, telephone interview by J. Cherie Strachan. Tape recording, September 2001.

47. Deborah O'Neil, "Dunedin Race Looks to Have 4 Candidates," *St. Petersburg Times*, Clearwater Times Section, 6 January 1999; Deborah O'Neil, "Candidates' Finance Reports Speak Volumes," *St. Petersburg Times*, Clearwater Times Section, 6 February 1999, 1; and Deborah O'Neil, "Kynes, Englebert Win Dunedin Seats," *St. Petersburg Times*, Clearwater Times Section, 10 February 1999, 1.

48. As quoted by Deborah O'Neil, "In Dunedin, Politics Ratchet Up," *St. Petersburg Times*, Clearwater Times Section, 2 February 2000, 1.

49. O'Neil, "In Dunedin, Politics Ratchet Up," 1.

50. O'Neil, "In Dunedin, Politics Ratchet Up," 1.

51. Deborah O'Neil, "Two Incumbents Retain Seats on Dunedin City Commission," *St. Petersburg Times*, Clearwater Times Section, 10 February 2000, 1.

52. As quoted by O'Neil, "In Dunedin, Politics Ratchet Up," 1.

53. As quoted by O'Neil, "In Dunedin, Politics Ratchet Up," 1.

54. Alexis de Tocqueville, *Democracy in America* (New York: Harper Perennial, 1969), 60.

55. For descriptions of such cultures, see Daniel J. Elazar, *American Federalism: A View from the States*, 2d ed. (New York: Thomas Y. Crowell, 1972), 99–102; and Robert D. Putnam, *Making Democracy Work: Civic Traditions in Modern Italy* (Princeton, N.J.: Princeton University Press, 1993).

56. Daniel Elazar, *Exploring Federalism* (Tuscaloosa: University of Alabama Press, 1987), 34–38.

57. Marion R. Just et al., *Crosstalk: Citizens, Candidates and the Media in a Presidential Election* (Chicago: University of Chicago Press, 1996), 235.

58. Anita Dunn, "The Best Campaign Wins: Local Press Coverage of Non-presidential Races," in *Campaigns and Elections American Style*, ed. James A. Thurber and Candice J. Nelson (Boulder, Colo.: Westview, 1995) 112.

59. Just et al., *Crosstalk*, 201.

60. Albany, N.Y., which meets both criteria, was excluded from the data set, as the city was used for exploratory research. In addition, the questions for the telephone interviews with local reporters were pretested with the local political reporter at the city's newspaper, the *Times Union*.

How Are Local Candidates Campaigning for Office?

2

Defying Conventional Wisdom in Bradenton, Florida

Conventional wisdom has logically predicted that sophisticated electoral tactics were unnecessary, and therefore unlikely, activities in electoral districts with smaller constituencies. Yet when former newspaper editor Wayne Poston challenged five-term incumbent Bill Evers in Bradenton, Florida, population 49,504, both candidates launched new-style campaigns, resulting in the most expensive mayoral race in the city's history.[1] Evers won a seat on the City Council in 1973 and had not lost a local election since.[2] In preparation for a serious fight, Poston began fundraising early, "quickly rivaling Evers in accumulating a hefty account of donations to finance a multi-media campaign."[3] Both candidates heeded the advice of campaign consultants and professional pollsters in developing campaign messages, which were communicated via traditional grassroots tactics such as yard signs and literature drops. The Poston campaign, for example, relied on assistance from more than 700 volunteers. Yet both candidates also turned to television spots and targeted direct mail.[4] Poston and Evers sent so much direct mail that an editorial in the local newspaper proclaimed, "To find their utility bills and pizza coupons, Bradenton residents have had to sift through mailboxes full of campaign fliers."[5] When the general election rolled around, $5.47 had been spent for each one of Bradenton's 29,345 registered voters.[6]

Despite these efforts, an "also-ran" candidate in the race, who received 10 percent of the vote, prevented either from winning a majority of the 9,059 ballots cast in the general election.[7] The result was a run-off, with Evers and Poston pulling out all the stops. Both raised additional funds of about $43,000, bringing Evers's total spending to $131,323 and Poston's to $112,673.[8] With about two weeks left before the run-off, Poston hired additional professional assistance to deliver critical votes in the city's African American precincts. Consultant Cynthia Fobbs, a Florida native who built her reputation working on Texas campaigns, proclaimed, "The votes we brought in made a difference."[9] The claim is hard to dispute, as Poston won the run-off election by a mere 774 votes. Evers received 4,463 votes, compared to Poston's 5,237.[10] After the Bradenton mayoral election, Fobbs opened a local consulting firm in Bradenton and was hired to work on a state legislative race.[11]

This account should pique the curiosity of those interested in the state of America's electoral processes. Does Poston's campaign strategy of supplementing a grassroots effort and ample volunteer support with sophisticated tactics and professional advice truly represent an isolated incident with implications only for the city of Bradenton? Or were his decisions part of a larger trend toward sophistication that might affect small-constituency electoral districts across the country? Both the mail survey of general consultants and the telephone interviews with local political reporters help to provide answers to such questions.

General Political Consultants Infiltrate Local Politics

Diverse Consultants Work on Local Races

The field of political consulting has expanded in the past two decades, resulting in diversity in both the regions of the country and the types of firms where political consultants are employed. The mail survey of general political consultants reflected this diversity, but revealed that it had no effect on which consultants worked for local candidates. Respondents to the mail survey worked in firms scattered across the United States. While California, Washington, D.C., and Virginia were still home to a plurality (39 percent) of these consultants, every major region of the country—including the South, the Midwest, the West, and the Northeast—was also represented. The consulting businesses where respondents worked also varied greatly in size, ranging from those having only 1 professional employee up to those with 150. One quarter of the respondents worked in businesses with only 1 professional employee, thereby suggesting that they are self-employed. Another 48 percent worked in small firms with 2 to 5 professional employees. Twenty-three percent worked in midsized firms with 6 to 20 such employees, while only 4 percent of the respondents worked in the largest firms, with 25 or more professional employees.

Despite these differences in the geographic location and size of firms, respondents served similar types of clients. When asked to indicate the population size of the electoral districts where they had worked, nearly all of the consultants (94 percent) indicated that they had worked for candidates running in districts with more than 250,000 residents. Yet high percentages of respondents also indicated that they had worked in smaller electoral districts with smaller populations. The percentage that claimed to have worked in midsized electoral districts—with populations between 50,000 and 99,999 residents; between 100,000 and 149,999 residents; and between 200,000 and 250,000 residents—ranged from 74 percent to 70 percent. Most revealing, however, is the finding that a full 76 percent of the respondents indicated that they had worked for candidates running for office in electoral districts with fewer than 50,000 residents. One respondent even noted in the margin of the questionnaire that he had worked for a candidate running for public office in a district with only 6,000 residents.[12]

Moreover, consultants worked with candidates in midsized electoral districts, irrespective of the location or size of their businesses. One might suspect, for example, given their proximity to the national government, that consultants headquartered in Washington, D.C., or nearby Virginia would focus on national or statewide races. Yet of the thirty respondents with headquarters near the Beltway, only 17 percent had never worked in a district with fewer than 250,000 residents. Meanwhile, 63 percent claimed to have worked in districts with fewer than 50,000 residents. Similarly, one might also suspect that consultants working in larger, more well-established firms would be less inclined to work on smaller races. Yet of the 9 consultants working in firms with 20 to 150 professional employees, only 3 had never worked in small-constituency races, whereas the remaining 6 had worked in districts with fewer than 50,000 residents. Even the 2 respondents working in firms with 150 other professionals claimed to have worked in races with smaller constituencies. On the other hand, none of the consultants working in these larger firms had failed to work for candidates in larger electoral districts.

Of the small minority of consultants who had never worked in large-constituency races, at least some appeared to focus on local government races by choice. Four of these 11 consultants may have been excluded from large-constituency races because of their lack of experience. The number of years that respondents had worked in the profession ranged from less than 1 up to 50 years, while the average length of their consulting careers was 17 years. Similarly, the most common length of the respondents' careers was 20 years. These 4 consultants had all worked as consultants for 6 or fewer years, and they all worked in businesses with only 1 or 2 professional employees. These circumstances suggest that they might have been trying to develop a reputation for winning local races in order to attract state and/or national candidates. Yet the remaining 7 consultants who had never worked in a district with more than 250,000 residents had lengthy careers, ranging from 12 to 21 years. Although 1 appeared to be self-employed, the remaining 6 worked at businesses with at least 3 and as many as 10 professional employees. Thus, a few consultants, although a small minority, appear to work exclusively in small-constituency races by choice.

A CORE GROUP OF LOCAL CONSULTANTS NOW EXISTS   Survey results suggest that even if consultants work for candidates in larger districts, they do not necessarily stop working with candidates in midsized ones. Although some high-visibility consultants make their living working exclusively for statewide and national candidates, responses to the questionnaire indicate that at least a core group of consultants now works with candidates in midsized local electoral districts.

Their Clients Incorporate Sophisticated Tactics

The fact that some local candidates have turned to political consultants is no guarantee that they have entirely embraced the trappings of new-style campaigns. Hence, the consultants who had worked with candidates in midsized electoral districts with fewer than 250,000 residents within the past two election cycles were asked to identify the tactics used throughout these campaigns.[13] Consultants' responses indicate that their local clientele relied on a broad array of tactics and activities. These are, in order from the most-used to the least-used tactic: direct mail (96 percent); free media coverage (92 percent); speeches (89 percent); telephone banks (87 percent); promotional products such as yard signs, T-shirts, or bumper stickers (83 percent); radio advertisements (81 percent); newspaper advertisements (79 percent); literature drops (79 percent); canvassing door-to-door (77 percent); debates (73 percent); public opinion polls (72 percent); television advertisements (68 percent); and Internet sites (40 percent).

All but one of these tactics are typically found in either old-style or new-style campaigns.[14] The traditional tactics of old-style campaigns rely either on less-sophisticated communication inventions or on grassroots activities requiring direct contact between candidates or their volunteers and the voters. The old-style tactics include earning free media coverage, giving speeches, participating in debates, canvassing door-to-door, distributing literature and promotional products, and using newspaper advertisements. Despite the involvement of consultants, whose expertise is typically required for the use of more sophisticated communication technology, these local government candidates did not abandon the traditional tactics of old-style campaigning, which appear to be an integral part of their campaigns.

While 92 percent and 89 percent of the consultants, respectively, indicated that their clients relied on earning free media coverage and giving speeches at local meetings, only a slightly smaller percentage said that their clients used promotional products. Meanwhile, the percentages of consultants with clients relying on newspaper advertisements, literature drops, and canvassing door-to-door were in the high 70s. In fact, the least-used traditional tactic of engaging in debates with opponents was reported by 73 percent of the consultants. With smaller constituencies, voters may know that direct contact with the candidates is feasible and may demand it. On the other hand, candidates and their consultants may cling to such tactics because they know that direct contact with candidates or their volunteers is the most effective way to persuade voters. In either case, turning to professional assistance has not led these candidates to abandon grassroots activities.

At the same time, consultants' responses indicate that their local clients have incorporated many of the sophisticated tactics of new-style campaigns, providing indirect contact with voters through communication technology. Rather than the resource of candidates' and volunteers' time that is so essential to grassroots activities, sophisticated tactics require the resource of money to purchase both the communication technology and the expertise typically needed to use it. Activities that can be classified as sophisticated tactics include television and radio advertisements, public opinion polls, targeted direct mail, and Internet sites.

By far the most popular sophisticated tactic, as well as the most popular tactic overall, was the use of targeted direct mail. Nearly all of the consultants (96 percent) indicated that this tactic was used by their local clientele. In comparison, only 81 percent of the consultants responded that clients used the next most common sophisticated tactic of radio advertisements. Yet radio advertisements were used more frequently than several grassroots activities such as newspaper advertisements, canvassing, literature drops, and debates. The remaining three sophisticated tactics were all used less frequently than any traditional tactic. Public opinion polling, one of the hallmarks of new-style campaigning, was used only slightly less frequently than debates, and television advertisements, reported by 68 percent of the consultants, were not far behind. In fact, the most notable finding concerns the limited use of Internet sites in comparison to all other sophisticated and traditional tactics.[15]

A LAYER OF SOPHISTICATED TACTICS SUPPLEMENTS TRADITIONAL EFFORTS Sophisticated tactics, such as direct mail and radio advertisements, were more widely used in these campaigns than were some traditional tactics. Yet the persuasive, grassroots activities so feasible with smaller constituencies were by no means abandoned. Instead of rejecting old-style campaign tactics, these local government candidates have added an additional layer of sophisticated activities to their traditional activities. This decision, whether based on voters' demands or candidates' insights, helps to preserve the direct contact between candidates and citizens that is praised by scholars as "an important part of the dialogue of democracy."[16]

Their Clients Hire Additional Professional Services

In addition to the specific types of tactics used in a campaign, the number of professionals hired to provide different services is an additional gauge of sophistication. General consultants can provide strategic advice, but they usually cannot provide a full array of sophisticated tactics on their own. With the development of new communication technologies, corresponding political consulting specialties emerged.[17] As the number of sophisticated tactics used by a candidate increases, the more professionals that person must hire to provide these. Hence, general consultants were also asked to identify the consulting specialists who were hired throughout these campaigns. Consultants reported that their local clientele hired various types of consulting specialists. They are, in order from the most-used to the least-used specialist: pollsters (70 percent), direct mail specialists (63 percent), television producers (54 percent), radio producers (50 percent), media buyers (38 percent), fundraisers (37 percent), demographic targeters (33 percent), lawyers (31 percent), volunteer trainers (7 percent), and telephone bank coordinators (4 percent). Seventy percent of the consultants indicated that their local clients hired pollsters, while 63 percent responded their clients hired direct mail specialists. Fifty-four percent and 50 percent of consultants, respectively, indicated that their recent local clients hired television and radio advertisement producers. A smaller number of consultants checked that their local government candidates relied on media buyers to purchase airtime on radio and television stations, paid fundraisers to raise money efficiently, used demographic targeters to describe the characteristics of voters in specific electoral districts, or hired lawyers to provide legal services. Finally, only a few responded that their clients needed additional assistance with building a telephone bank or training their volunteers.

Interestingly, the type of specialist most frequently hired does not correspond to the most popular type of sophisticated tactic. Far more consultants indicated that their clients relied on targeted direct mail than on public opinion polling. Yet 70 percent indicated that their candidates hired pollsters, and only 63 percent claimed to use direct mail specialists. This difference can be attributed to how difficult it is for general consultants to possess the resources and to master the skills needed to provide each type of service. Successful public opinion polling requires access to trained interviewers, computers, and telephones for the interviewing process. A great deal of skill is required not only to write questions measuring voters' attitudes, but to accurately interpret statistical findings. Producing and mailing effective direct mail pieces also requires specialized skills, such as producing eye-catching mailers and developing a list of appropriate addresses. Yet these skills require less training to master than do survey research methods. Moreover, they can be performed by people with access to a personal computer and relatively inexpensive software programs.

The relationships between the number of consultants reporting that their clients used sophisticated tactics and the number indicating that a corresponding specialist was hired support the supposition that specialists are relied on most heavily when they offer services that are difficult for nonexperts to replicate. As expected, the strongest relationship to hiring a specialist occurred when clients used public opinion polls. Seventy-nine percent of the consultants whose local clients used public opinion polling also indicated that a pollster was hired. The second strongest association was found not with use of direct mail, but with television advertisements. Sixty-nine percent of the consultants whose local clients used television advertisements also reported that a television producer was hired. This result makes sense, as producing a quality television commercial requires access to specialized filming and editing equipment, as well as the ability to use them. Meanwhile, the relationship between using direct mail and hiring a direct mail specialist was a close third, at 63 percent. The association between using a radio advertisement and hiring a radio producer was 58 percent. Finally, the weakest relationships were found for using either a television or a radio advertisement and hiring a media buyer. Only 45 percent of the consultants whose local clients used television advertisements reported that a media buyer was hired, and the relationship to the use of radio advertisements was 42 percent. Again, this finding makes sense because buying time on radio and television stations requires no special equipment, and the skills needed to do so can be easily learned through research and firsthand experiences.

These findings suggest an explanation for the reason so few of the consultants' local clients turned to professional assistance for volunteer training or coordination of telephone banks, despite the frequent use of grassroots activities and telephone banks in their campaigns. For example, the relationship between using literature drops and hiring a volunteer trainer was only 9 percent, and just 4 percent of the general consultants' local clients using a telephone phone bank had also hired a coordinator. The reason behind these weak relationships is that these types of activities do not require specialized skills and can be performed by either a general consultant or a volunteer with past campaign experience.

PROFESSIONAL SERVICES UNDERSCORE SOPHISTICATION OF LOCAL EFFORTS   Yet a majority of these consultants' local clients relied on some form of additional professional assistance. The complexity of public opinion polling and the frequent use of direct mail made specialists in these two tactics particularly popular. Other findings show that specialists are relied on most heavily when nonexperts would have difficulty performing the services that specialists offer. These local clients' reliance on additional professional services in specific areas underscores the sophistication of their campaigns. They were willing to hire additional expertise for their campaigns in order to guarantee the successful use of particularly complex, sophisticated tactics associated with new-style campaign strategies.

Local Clients Are More Than Just Mayoral Candidates

Enough candidates in midsized electoral districts have turned to new-style campaign activities to employ a core group of general political consultants. Yet one might expect that only certain types of local candidates are hiring these consultants. For example, it may seem that candidates running for executive offices, such as mayor or county executive, would seek out professional assistance. These races typically have higher visibility and a larger electorate than other local government positions. As a result, they may attract more aggressive candidates, with the ability to raise money from a larger pool of potential donors. To determine whether only specific types of local government candidates are turning to new-style campaigns and professional assistance, general consultants were asked to identify the types of candidates for whom they had worked in the past two election cycles. Table 2.1 reveals the percentages of consultants reporting that they had recently worked for specific types of local candidates.

These consultants had recently worked in a broad array of local races. More consultants worked for candidates for local legislative office than for any other type of candidate, as 74 percent had worked for county legislators and 61 percent for city council members. This finding simply reflects the fact that local legislative positions are more numerous than other types of local elective offices, not that local legislative candidates are more likely to run new-style campaigns. Candidates for mayor were frequent clients, as 57 per-

Table 2.1   Consultants' Presence across the Spectrum of Local Races

Local Office	% of Consultants with Recent Clients	Local Office	% of Consultants with Recent Clients
County Races		*Municipal Races*	
Legislator	74	Council Member	61
Judge	43	Mayor	57
Commissioner	40	Judge	26
Executive	34	*Special Districts Races*	
Sheriff	26	School Board	12
Prosecuting Attorney	23	Other	6

N = 151.
Source: 1998 mail survey of general political consultants.

cent of the consultants had recently worked for them. Substantial numbers of consultants also conducted campaigns for county judge, commissioner, and executive candidates. Meanwhile, the percentages of consultants reporting that they had worked for county sheriffs, prosecuting attorneys, and city judges ranged from 23 percent to 26 percent. A few consultants indicated that they had worked in school board and other special district races. The diversity of the respondents' local clientele is further illustrated by the list generated from their additional comments. It includes clerk of courts, register of wills, recorder, tax collector, assessor, controller, town supervisor, town council member, selectman (an administrator elected by voters in New England town meetings), and elections inspector. A few had even worked for people seeking positions within political party organizations.

SOPHISTICATION OCCURS ACROSS THE SPECTRUM OF LOCAL RACES   Although the number of consultants working on such races in the past is unknown, clearly consultants are now making a presence across the entire spectrum of local government races. They are being hired by candidates running for prominent local public offices, as well as by those running for less well-known positions. On occasion, they have even helped people seeking positions within the political parties. Yet the format of the questionnaire did not ask consultants to specify the campaign tactics used by each type of local candidate for whom they had worked. Thus, consultants who had worked for several types of local candidates would have checked the sophisticated tactics and additional professional services, even if these activities were used only by their clients running for executive office.

To address this concern, 10 respondents who had worked only for candidates running for less-visible local government candidates were identified. Of these 10 consultants, only 1, whose only local clientele were selectmen in Massachusetts, indicated that his clients had used no sophisticated tactics or professional services. Of the remaining 9 consultants, 9 had clients who used direct mail, 6 had clients who used both public opinion polling and radio advertisements, 4 had clients who used television advertisements, and 2 had clients with Internet sites. These 9 consultants also reported that their clients had relied on additional professional services. Seven had clients who hired direct mail specialists, 6 had clients who hired pollsters, 4 had clients who hired television producers, and 2 had clients who hired radio producers. Of additional interest, 1 of these 9 consultants' only local clients were candidates for town supervisor and town council, and he indicated that they had relied on all available communication technologies except the Internet, as well as on professional assistance with polling and production of radio and television advertisements.

While the survey results cannot be used to make generalized claims about the overall population of local government candidates, the data gathered reveal that new-style campaign tactics, including the use of professional assistance, have been adopted by many different types of candidates for local elected offices.

Consultants Charge Affordable Fees

One characteristic shared by general consultants' diverse clientele may be access to plentiful campaign funds. Without money, candidates cannot afford to purchase campaign technology or to hire the specialists who know how to use it. To determine whether new-style campaigns were an option only for exceptionally well-funded local government candidates, the general consultants were asked to estimate their fees. Respondents were provided with a list of potential fees in $2,500 increments up to $10,000 and in $5,000 increments up to $80,000, and they were asked to select the amount most closely representing their fees for providing services to recent local candidates throughout the duration of their campaigns.

Seven consultants either donated their services or charged less than $1,000, while two consultants charged more than $80,000 for their services. The remaining responses ranged from $2,500 to $60,000, with the bulk of the responses clustered from the middle to the low end of the scale. Thirty-two percent of the respondents charged $7,500 or less for their services, and another 48 percent charged between $10,000 and $25,000. Thirteen percent charged between $30,000 and $40,000 for their services, but only 7 percent charged the highest fees of $45,000 or more. The average fee charged by these consultants was $17,700. It should be noted that including the small number of high fees in this calculation inflates the average fee. For example the most popular fee, charged by 17 percent of the respondents, was only $5,000.

In addition, particular regions of the country are not characterized by either high or low consulting fees. One of the consultants charging fees of over $80,000 was located in California, and the other worked in Pennsylvania. The remaining thirteen consultants charging comparatively high fees, ranging from $45,000 to $60,000, had headquarters in states scattered across the country.[18] The twelve consultants charging the most affordable fees, from donated services to $2,500, could also be found in every major region of the country.[19]

FEES MAKE LOCAL SOPHISTICATION FEASIBLE   The cost of purchasing the trappings of new-style campaigns will still drive up local campaign budgets. Communication technologies and professional assistance, even if now more affordable, still cost more than grassroots activities. While local candidates may need to raise additional money to adopt sophisticated tactics, these results reveal that it is now feasible for many local government candidates to raise sufficient funds to hire a general political consultant.

Summary of Consultants' Insights

In summary, these results reveal that a sufficient number of candidates in midsized electoral districts have begun using sophisticated tactics and professional assistance to employ at least a core group of general political consultants. These findings contradict the conventional wisdom that candidates with smaller constituencies, who can more feasibly undertake persuasive grassroots activities, would find new-style campaign activities unnecessary. In addition, the use of communication technology and professional assistance is not limited to a specific type of local government candidate. While providing these broad insights, the mail survey alone fails to give an account of how widespread the use of sophisticated tactics by local government candidates has become since it describes only the campaigns run by local government candidates who hired a general consultant. The sophistication of their campaigns may not be a reflection of all local government candidates' campaigns.

New-Style Campaigning in Midsized Cities across the United States

Reporters Describe Use of Sophisticated Tactics

Information gathered from telephone interviews with local political reporters provides a better indicator of how widespread new-style campaigns have become; this information can be used to develop a descriptive account of campaigns in a particular subset of local government elections. Unlike the mail survey, questions were asked about all mayoral candidates in midsized cities, regardless of whether they turned to professional assistance. In addition to providing this specific descriptive account, information about the sophistication of mayoral campaigns can be used to make predictions about that of other local government races. If competitive mayoral candidates in a given city have not adopted new-style campaigns, it is unlikely that other municipal candidates will have adopted them.

According to reporters, mayoral candidates are using a broad array of campaign tactics in their efforts to win public office. When the researcher gathered this information, reporters were read a series of campaign tactics and asked to indicate those used by the mayoral candidates in their respective city. They are, in order from the most- to the least-used tactic: speeches (97 percent), yard signs (96 percent), literature drops (95 percent), newspaper advertisements (89 percent), canvassing (83 percent), direct mail (79 percent), telephone banks (69 percent), radio advertisements (62 percent), tele-vision advertisements (47 percent), public opinion polls (41 percent), and Internet sites (16 percent).[20] This list is noticeably different from the one describing the tactics used by general consultants' local clients. Those used most frequently by general consultants' local clients included a mix of sophis-ticated and traditional tactics. Recall that direct mail was the most popular tactic and that radio advertisements—the sixth most popular tactic—were used more often than were several traditional activities. The list generated from reporters' responses, however, can be clearly divided into traditional and sophisticated activities. The five activities that mayoral candidates used the most are all traditional. Meanwhile, with the exception of telephone banks, the last five on the list are all sophisticated.

Reporters' accounts reveal that mayoral candidates relied heavily on tradi-tional activities. Speeches, yard signs, and literature drops were nearly univer-sal tactics. Most also relied on newspaper advertisements and canvassed door-to-door. Mayoral candidates were more reliant on every traditional tactic than were the local political candidates who hired general consultants. In fact, most mayoral candidates relied on all of the available traditional tactics. Sev-enty-four percent, for example, used all five of these traditional tactics, and another 17 percent used four. Only 9 percent used three or fewer traditional tactics in their campaigns.

Similarly, mayoral candidates were also less reliant on every sophisticated tactic. These findings support the assumption that the sophistication of cam-paigns waged with the assistance of a general consultant do not reflect all local election campaigns. Yet the comparison should not overshadow the fact that significant numbers of mayoral candidates have incorporated sophisti-cated tactics into their campaign strategies. Well over a majority of the candi-dates relied on direct mail and radio advertisements, while 47 percent used television advertisements, and 41 percent relied on public opinion polls. Only 16 percent, however, had Internet sites.[21]

MOST MAYORAL CANDIDATES HAVE ADOPTED NEW-STYLE TAC-TICS   Although mayoral candidates in midsized cities are more reliant on traditional, grassroots activities, many have also launched new-style cam-paigns. Summarizing their use of these sophisticated tactics underscores this point. (Internet sites were excluded from this summary because it was not clear that candidates were using them in a manner consistent with new-style campaigning.) Eighty-eight percent of the mayoral candidates used at least one sophisticated tactic in their respective campaigns, while only 19 percent used just one. Meanwhile, 27 percent relied on two sophisticated tactics, and nearly as many used three. Far fewer relied on more than three sophisticated tactics, but 19 percent of mayoral candidates managed to incorporate all four sophisticated tactics—polls, television ads, targeted direct mail, and radio ads—in their campaigns. Thus 69 percent of the mayoral candidates relied on multiple sophisticated tactics in their efforts to win office.

Reporters Describe Reliance on Professional Services

Not surprisingly, given their adoption of sophisticated tactics, some mayoral candidates have also turned to assistance from campaign professionals. When the researcher gathered this information, reporters were read a list of campaign professionals and asked to identify those hired by mayoral candidates. In some cases, a single professional provided more than one service. For example, a campaign's media producer may have also served as its media buyer. Therefore, the list represents the types of professional services purchased, rather than the absolute number of professionals hired.

They are, in order from the most-used to the least-used professional service: media producers (40 percent), pollsters (35 percent), direct mail specialists (34 percent), campaign managers (32 percent), media buyers (25 percent), demographic targeters (18 percent), accountants (10 percent), attorneys (9 percent), fundraisers (8 percent), and volunteer trainers (4 percent). Again, mayoral candidates were less reliant on all types of professional services than were the local government candidates described by general political consultants. Yet the numbers of mayoral candidates turning to political consultants are too large to disregard. The most popular professionals, media producers, were hired by 40 percent of the mayoral candidates. Meanwhile, the percentage of candidates hiring pollsters, direct mail specialists, and campaign managers ranged from 35 percent to 32 percent. Eighteen percent hired a demographic targeter, and 10 percent or fewer relied on accountants, attorneys, fundraisers, or volunteer trainers.

Again, the types of specialists most frequently hired do not correspond to the most popular types of sophisticated tactics. While direct mail was the most popular sophisticated tactic, mayoral candidates were more apt to hire the expertise of media producers and pollsters. As with the local government candidates described by general consultants, mayoral candidates turned to specialists more frequently as the complexity of their services increased. In fact, the relationships between using a particular tactic and hiring a corresponding specialist mirror those discovered by the mail survey of general consultants. Candidates using public opinion polls were the most apt to hire a specialist. Eighty-eight percent of the mayoral candidates who used a poll also hired a pollster. The second-strongest relationship was found for the use of television advertisements, as 72 percent of the candidates using this tactic hired a media producer. Forty-two percent of those using direct mail hired a specialist, and 30 percent of those using radio advertisements hired a media producer.[22]

MOST MAYORAL CANDIDATES HAVE HIRED PROFESSIONAL CON-
SULTANTS   Many mayoral candidates using sophisticated tactics hired the
expertise of consulting specialists in their campaigns. Their willingness to seek
out additional professional assistance to guarantee the successful use of particularly complex tactics underscores the sophistication of their campaigns.
Only 36 percent of mayoral candidates ran for office without the benefit of
expert assistance, and most relied on multiple professional services. While 19
percent of mayoral candidates relied on one professional service, 12 percent
used two, and another 12 percent had three. Far fewer candidates relied on
more than three professionals. For example, combining the categories of
four, five, or six services purchased accounts for only 17 percent of the mayoral candidates. Finally, only 4 percent relied on more than six services. Yet a
minority of candidates in midsized cities amassed an impressive array of campaign professionals. In addition, well over one-half of mayoral candidates
purchased at least one professional service during the course of their campaigns.

Conclusion

These descriptive accounts reveal that elements of new-style campaigns have
filtered into campaigns for local government offices. At some point, candidates in midsized electoral districts began incorporating sophisticated tactics
and professional assistance into their efforts to win public office. At least a
core group of general political consultants is hired by such candidates. Meanwhile, in the most recent mayoral elections in America's midsized cities, 69
percent of the candidates used two or more sophisticated tactics, and 64 percent purchased the expertise of at least one campaign professional. These candidates have not abandoned traditional tactics, but many have added layers
of sophistication and professionalism to their campaign strategies.

Although this chapter reveals that new-style campaigns are taking place in
America's midsized electoral districts, it makes no attempt to explain why
some local government candidates have adopted this approach. Yet the phenomenon of new-style local campaigns is intriguing. Unlike candidates running in larger districts, many local government candidates can effectively
reach most of the members of their electorate through traditional activities.
In many midsized cities, it is possible to meet most of the voting public in
person by attending events or canvassing door-to-door, and, with a limited
number of volunteers, campaign literature can be hand-delivered to all of the
voters in the district. Yet candidates are also relying on electronic advertisements. It is easier to assess voters' concerns in a smaller, more homogeneous
district, but local government candidates are still turning to public opinion
polls. Given these circumstances, the question that begs to be asked is: What
motivates local government candidates to adopt sophisticated tactics that

often require assistance from professionals? This question will be addressed in chapter 3, which explores how candidates who use such activities differ from those who do not.

Notes

1. "The Cost of Campaigning," *The Bradenton Herald,* 24 October 1999, 7(B).

2. "Fiercely Fought Campaign Nears End," *The Bradenton Herald,* 24 October 1999, 1(B).

3. "Fiercely Fought Campaign Nears End," 1(B).

4. Gretchen Parker, "Evers Claims Poll Contributed to Rival," *Sarasota Herald Tribune,* Manatee Edition, 15 October 1999, 1(B); "Evers' Survey Draws Protest," *Sarasota Herald Tribune,* Manatee Edition, 19 October 1999, 1(B); "Mayoral Slugfest in Hands of Voters," *Sarasota Herald Tribune,* Manatee Edition, 2 November 1999, 1(B); and Gretchen Parker, "Wayne Poston Sworn in as Bradenton Mayor," *Sarasota Herald Tribune,* Manatee Edition, 5 January 2000, 1(A).

5. "Mayoral Slugfest in Hands of Voters," 1(B).

6. "Mayoral Slugfest in Hands of Voters," 1(B).

7. "Message for the Mayor," *Sarasota Herald Tribune,* Manatee Edition, 3 November 1999, 1(B).

8. "Contributions Listed," *Sarasota Herald Tribune,* Manatee Edition, 20 November 1999, 1(B).

9. Yvette Kim, "African-American Firm Enters Local Political Scene," *Sarasota Herald Tribune,* Manatee Edition, 4 February 2000, 4(B).

10. Gretchen Parker, "End of an Era," *Sarasota Herald Tribune,* Manatee Edition, 24 November 1999, 1(A).

11. Christopher Cole, "Bradenton, Fla., Campaign Aids Open Political Consulting Firm," *The Bradenton Herald,* 19 January 2000, 2(A).

12. This comment, as well as the finding that many consultants have worked in localities with even fewer than 50,000 residents, suggests that future research should explore the adoption of new-style campaign activities in even smaller districts than addressed here.

13. A total of 159 respondents had worked with candidates in midsized localities in the past two election cycles.

14. Phone banks can be conducted traditionally with a room full of donated phones and volunteers, or they can be quite sophisticated with computer-assisted dialing and highly trained staff. Unfortunately, the questionnaire did not ask consultants to specify the way their clients' phone banks were conducted.

15. This finding may simply be a result of the novelty of this tactic in all types of campaigns at the time the survey was conducted.

16. Paul S. Herrnson, "Field Work, Political Parties, and Volunteerism," in *Campaigns and Elections American Style,* ed. James A. Thurber and Candice J. Nelson (Boulder, Colo.: Westview, 1995), 160.

17. Robert V. Friedenberg, *Communication Consultants in Political Campaigns* (Westport, Conn.: Praeger, 1997), 24.

18. These states are California, Florida, Maryland, New York, Nevada, Ohio, Tennessee, Virginia, and Washington, as well as Washington, D.C.

19. These states are Arizona, California, Massachusetts, Missouri, North Carolina, New Jersey, New York, and Ohio, as well as Washington, D.C.

20. Some of the tactics mentioned by general political consultants and included on the list of tactics used by their clients are missing from this list. This discrepancy occurred because many consultants took the opportunity to write additional tactics on their questionnaires, and their additions were included in the findings.

21. Again, the limited use of the Internet may result from the novelty of this tactic at the time the interviews were conducted

22. Since the telephone interviews asked only about media producers, rather than about television and radio producers separately, the relationship between using radio advertisements and hiring a media producer was found by controlling for the use of television advertisements.

Why Are Local Candidates Adopting New-Style Campaign Strategies?

3

Explaining Campaign Sophistication in Annapolis, Maryland

Annapolis, Maryland, population 35,838, has been described as a small town at heart, as a place where candidates are not abstract images on a television screen, but familiar members of the community. The city is small enough that people often run into local public officials at the drugstore or local carry-out, and many claim that registered voters can be reached with a door-to-door canvass.[1] Yet the candidates in Annapolis are "turning increasingly to TV ads, pollsters, targeted mass mailings and professional campaign managers to reach voters."[2] In the city's 1997 mayoral race, where term limits resulted in an open seat, the use of such sophisticated tactics began in the primaries. An account of the election provides several potential explanations for the use of new-style campaigns at the local level.

In the Democratic primary, a three-term council member, Carl O. Snowden, faced former mayor Dennis Callahan. Snowden spent $80,000 on a variety of new-style tactics. His first step was to hire a campaign manager known for her work on campaigns across the country. With her guidance, as well as with information gleaned from public opinion polling, messages were targeted to particular constituencies via telephone banks, direct mail, an Internet site, and radio and cable television advertisements. Underscoring the sophistication of his campaign effort, Snowden relied on the expertise of firms specializing in direct mail, polling, push polling, and media production. When asked to explain his campaign decisions, Snowden pointed out that the increasing number of commuters living in Annapolis has made knocking on doors a less effective way to reach voters.[3]

Snowden's opponent in the primary spent only $23,000, but still managed to incorporate several sophisticated tactics into his campaign. Callahan was spared the expense of a professional pollster when a campaign supporter passed on the results of a public opinion poll. Skilled acquaintances also

37

helped with the production of cable television ads and with demographic targeting for direct-mail pieces. Meanwhile, Callahan, who had hired out-of-state consultants in his losing 1993 campaign, felt comfortable coordinating these efforts himself. When asked why local candidates feel the need to adopt sophisticated efforts, Callahan pointed out that consultants providing such services "come out of the woodwork" seeking clients, especially in off-year races.[4]

Callahan downplayed the need to spend large amounts of money in local races, instead emphasizing the importance of favorable earned media coverage. At the same time, he acknowledged that candidates must raise enough to be perceived as viable alternatives.[5] Those who do not may suffer the fate of a third candidate in the 1997 Democratic primary, Sylvanus Jones, who was described by the press as an "under-financed longshot."[6] Jones, along with his wife and son, canvassed the city extensively. During the campaign, he claimed, "I'm using my time wisely, I'm using my shoe leather wisely. That will have better results than all the money in the world."[7] A candidate seeking the Republican nomination even observed, "There isn't a house Sylvanus has missed. Everywhere I go, he's been there before me."[8] Press coverage of Jones's efforts, however, emphasized his lack of a campaign headquarters, of a campaign staff, and of money to finance his race.[9]

Callahan won the Democratic primary with 1,567 of the votes cast—Snowden pulled in 1,399 votes, with Jones receiving 680—and he went to face Republican Dean Johnson in the general election.[10] Johnson had incorporated some sophisticated tactics in the Republican primary, including a professional public opinion poll, targeted mailings produced by a direct-mail firm, and radio advertisements. To face Callahan in the general election, Johnson hired a consultant with experience in congressional campaigns and added cable television spots to his campaign efforts. One might suspect that Johnson added these tactics because he felt pressured to match the activities of his opponent. Yet he explained local candidates' use of new-style tactics with the simple statement, "Around here, voters are expecting it."[11] Despite being outspent by Callahan $30,000 to $40,000 in the general election, Johnson won the race 4,127 to 3,416.[12]

Candidates' Shifting Notions of Campaigns

This account of candidates in Annapolis illustrates how a growing number of local candidates have started to think about campaigning, as they adopt increasingly sophisticated tactics. Their decisions to do so are not driven by necessity, because a straightforward analysis of the benefits such candidates can hope to gain from sophisticated tactics suggests that they would be content to rely on more traditional grassroots activities. Yet their notion of what constitutes a serious, local political campaign no longer corresponds with the activities of old-style campaigning. Insight into this shift comes by understanding how people process political information and make decisions based on it. People abstract information from their personal or vicarious experiences to create a mental image or a schema, which hierarchically organizes information about situations and individuals. Each schema includes a conception of a general pattern, as well as a limited number of illustrative examples. This cognitive structure is used to process and store new information or to retrieve existing information.[13] Once in place, a schema is used to shape expectations for appropriate events and actions in a particular circumstance. Hence, when people have a well-developed schema for a local election, "they can envision the characters in such scenarios, the props, the actions, and the sequence of actions."[14] One of schemata's major functions is to help people solve problems and make decisions. By providing information about "likely scenarios and ways to cope with them," schemata are "an important element in deciding whether to act and how to act."[15] Consequently, when local candidates' schema of a successful local campaign corresponds to old-style campaigning, they will be content to rely on traditional tactics. Yet if a schema corresponds to new-style campaigns, relying solely on traditional tactics would be perceived as an inadequate campaign effort. Some of the characters, props, and actions, such as consultants, communication technologies, and sophisticated tactics, envisioned in their scenario of a successful local campaign would be missing. Once a new-style schema of local campaigns has been established, candidates will use it to decide what activities should be included in their campaign strategies. Where polls and television commercials would once have been considered extraneous or perhaps even inappropriate campaign activities, they now come to be seen as necessities. Although the Annapolis candidates speculated about potential reasons for this shift, the question that remains to be answered with empirical data is: What leads such local candidates to develop a new-style campaign schema and to adopt sophisticated tactics?

Several potential influences should be explored. On one hand, candidates' decisions may be driven by their personal traits and experiences. Certain types of people may simply be more inclined to turn to sophisticated efforts than others are. On the other hand, candidates may be driven to innovate in an effort to meet local community expectations about appropriate campaign strategies. In addition to these two possibilities, the structures of the local political environment that affect candidates' chances for success may determine whether local candidates decide to alter their electoral efforts. Determining which, if any, of these factors shape candidates' adoption decisions is essential to understanding the phenomenon of new-style local campaigns. Without an explanation of why candidates change their approach, the permanence of the trend cannot be predicted, and efforts to influence it cannot be evaluated.

To provide this important insight, the sophistication of mayoral candidates' campaigns will be compared. In order to undertake this comparison, the numbers of new-style campaign tactics each candidate used were simply added together.[16] A defining trait of new-style campaigns is that they incorporate an array of advanced communication efforts. As imitation of this campaigning style is achieved, the number of sophisticated tactics a candidate employs should increase. These summaries of candidates' campaign efforts counted four sophisticated tactics—the use of public opinion polls, television ads, targeted direct mail, and radio ads—all of which were associated with hiring consultants. Internet sites, which obviously incorporate new communication technology, are notably absent from this list. As previously indicated, the novelty of Internet sites at the time the data were collected probably resulted in limited use. It was also unclear from survey responses whether the small number of candidates using Internet sites were apt to hire experts to create and manage them. Unlike the remaining four sophisticated tactics, no clear pattern between using Internet sites and hiring additional professional services was documented. Hence, the decision was made to exclude Internet sites from the summaries.

Table 3.1 serves as a reminder that substantial numbers of mayoral candidates have incorporated each of these four key sophisticated tactics into their campaigns, and that many have also used several such tactics in their electoral efforts. The second column of this table lists the percentage of mayoral candidates using each type of tactic, while the fourth column lists the percentage of candidates using multiple sophisticated tactics in their efforts. Regardless of the fact that these candidates also maintained reliance on grassroots activities, table 3.1 indicates that many have adopted the tactics characteristic of new-style campaigns.

The simple summaries of campaign sophistication constructed for each candidate weight each of the four tactics equally. Some tactics, however, rely on communication technology that is both more complex and more difficult

Table 3.1   Mayoral Candidates' Use of Sophisticated Tactics

Type of Tactic	% of Candidates	Number of Tactics	% of Candidates
Polls	41	Zero	12
Television Ads	47	One	19
Targeted Direct Mail	79	Two	27
Radio Ads	62	Three	23
		Four	19

Source: 1998 interviews about the most recent mayoral candidates in midsized cities.

to master. Hence, as a campaign's sophistication increases, so should the use of more complex tactics such as public opinion polls and television ads. Yet weighting particular tactics more heavily than others proved to be unnecessary because most candidates who were capable of incorporating the most sophisticated campaign activities also used simpler ones. For example, of all the candidates who used public opinion polls, only two failed to use additional sophisticated tactics. Meanwhile, all of the candidates whose most complex tactic was a television advertisement relied on direct mail and/or radio advertisements. Since the candidates with the most complex tactics also relied on a higher total number of tactics, the simple summary of tactics used accurately reflects levels of campaign sophistication. (See appendix B to review a complete reproduction of the naturally scaled order of this data.)

Moving beyond Conventional Wisdom

Before examining other influences on campaign sophistication, we should acknowledge the partial explanation of new-style campaigns provided by conventional wisdom. As conventional wisdom predicts, a relationship exists between the use of sophisticated tactics and electorate size, as candidates with larger electorates employ more sophisticated types of communication technology. For example, of the mayoral candidates in midsized cities, 70 percent of those running in cities with more than 150,000 residents relied on the most sophisticated tactic of public opinion polls, whereas the tactic was used by only 35 percent of other mayoral candidates. This relationship, however, should not be overstated because conventional wisdom is less accurate in predicting the use of less-complex sophisticated tactics. Seventy percent of the candidates in the larger cities used radio, but so did 60 percent of those in smaller ones. The difference between those relying on television is slightly more. Fifty-nine percent of mayoral candidates in cities with more than 150,000 residents used television advertisements, but so did 46 percent of the remaining candidates. Yet this pattern of use is reversed when considering targeted direct mail. While 77 percent of the candidates in larger cities used the tactic, 80 percent of those with smaller districts followed suit.

As the number of people whom candidates must contact increases, so do the benefits to be gained from relying on advanced communication technology. Thus population size must be taken into consideration when attempting to explain the phenomenon of new-style local campaigns. Obviously, however, electorate size provides only one piece of the puzzle. The weak relationship discovered for all but one of these sophisticated tactics indicates that population alone cannot account for local candidates' adoption of sophisticated campaign tactics.

Consultants Discredit the Importance of Population Size

This finding is underscored by the opinions of general political consultants. In the mail survey, general consultants were provided with a list of potential influences on their clients' decisions to adopt new campaign tactics and were asked to select the most important one. Notably, only a solitary consultant believed that the population size of the electorate was most influential. Advances in communication technology enabling consultants to target small groups of voters appear to have diminished the importance of this consideration.

On the other hand, 41 percent of the consultants identified themselves as the most important influence on their clients' decisions. Numerous consultants expanded on this selection by explaining that they were hired precisely because they could provide such guidance. One consultant wrote, "People hire consultants for advice and generally follow that advice," and another indicated, "Once they [the candidates] hire us, they are already committed to a professional effort." A third consultant provided a more in-depth explanation with the following note: "Most candidates, at some point, realize that they don't understand the winning process in . . . developing a campaign. At that point, they realize the value of a 'professional's' advice." In short, their clients were interested in running new-style campaigns and wanted professional guidance about which sophisticated tactics would be effective in their particular districts and circumstances.

The second-most frequently selected factor, chosen by 28 percent of the consultants, was the availability of campaign funds. Obviously, financial constraints may prevent candidates and their consultants from adopting desired tactics. Communication technology cannot be used if candidates cannot afford to pay for it. These two influences, consultants' advice and budgetary constraints, affect candidates' use of sophisticated tactics, but not the initial inclination to adopt them. Candidates hire specialists to help them after they have decided to move beyond grassroots efforts. Budget limitations may prevent them from incorporating some sophisticated tactics. Yet these influences occur after the commitment to a new-style campaign strategy has occurred.

Other factors, chosen by smaller numbers of political consultants, would influence candidates' decisions to turn to new-style strategies in the first place. For example, 13 percent of the consultants believed that the tactics used by prior successful candidates were most important in their candidates' adoption decisions. Meanwhile, 5 percent chose the personality or style of the candidate, and another 5 percent selected the closeness of the race.[17] Perhaps it is not a coincidence that these three factors mirror the potential influences on adoption decisions outlined previously. Hence, the insights they contribute into the phenomenon of new-style local campaigns will be explored next.

The Influence of Candidates' Characteristics and Personal Experiences

Personal experiences often affect potential adopters' willingness to adopt new technology. Quite simply, people often do not become dissatisfied with their current practices until after learning about a new alternative.[18] "Thus knowledge of the existence of an innovation can create motivation for its adoption."[19] Perhaps personal experiences that increase local candidates' familiarity with communication technology encourage them to go sophisticated, despite the smaller sizes of their electoral districts.

Does a Cosmopolitan Network of Associates Matter?

Typical innovators of any new type of technology in a particular community are more cosmopolitan than others. Their personal and professional networks of contacts extend outside their own localities, as they "travel widely and are involved in matters beyond the boundaries of their local system."[20] Granted, political candidates are often members of the political elite and are thus more apt to be cosmopolitan than are potential adopters of other types of technologies. Yet diversity within the population of local government candidates still exists. Some, perhaps those who aspire to state or national offices, will have broader networks than others.

These types of external interactions may be what lead cosmopolitan local government candidates to begin altering their local campaign schema. Without these networks, candidates are limited to developing their schema of a local campaign from observations of or experiences in the previous campaigns for office conducted within their own communities. If all the candidates in a particular local political arena are provincial, none would glean the information about new-style campaign alternatives needed to alter their schema. All local candidates are surely aware that advanced communication technology has been used in political campaigns. News coverage of presidential, U.S. Senate, and gubernatorial races often emphasizes candidates' use of public opinion polls and the electronic media. Yet this awareness is not as persuasive as direct contact with other experienced politicians. News coverage does not provide information about the ways that communication technology can be adapted to reach small audiences. It does not explain how to go about contacting professional political consultants, how to hire a qualified pollster, or what types of fees such professionals might charge local clients. General awareness of communication technology may be insufficient to alter candidates' local campaign schema.

A cosmopolitan candidate with a wider range of political networks would be exposed to candidates, particularly those serving in larger districts, who could provide this type of persuasive information. By sharing their campaign stories, explaining the benefits of more sophisticated tactics, and providing advice, these external contacts could provide local candidates with the vicarious experiences that lead them to adopt more sophisticated campaign tactics. Thus, one might expect cosmopolitan local candidates to be more apt to have new-style campaigns than provincial local candidates are.

Each mayoral candidate's degree of cosmopolitanness was measured with two questions. First, a question was posed to gauge the presence of cosmopolitan networks. Reporters were read the following paragraph and asked to consider how accurately it described each mayoral candidate in their city:

> Some local candidates have a wide array of friends and professional acquaintances. They enjoy and seek out contact with people who live outside their local community, including state or national party officials and elected officials. As a result, they have many personal and professional associations with people who live elsewhere.

Second, to check the accuracy of this measure, reporters were asked an additional question intended to measure provincialism or the absence of cosmopolitan networks. They were read the following paragraph and again asked to indicate whether it was only slightly, somewhat, fairly, or very accurate of each mayoral candidate in their city:

> Other local candidates have a smaller number of friends and professional acquaintances. Most of the people they seek out, including party officials and elected officials, are members of their local community. They are content to have primarily local personal and professional associations.

Reporters' responses to these two questions reveal a great deal of perceived variety in mayoral candidates' contact with outside friends and acquaintances. Reporters indicated that the first paragraph was a very accurate description of 23 percent of the candidates, fairly accurate of 21 percent, somewhat accurate of 31 percent, and only slightly accurate of 25 percent. Surprisingly, the responses to the second paragraph do not mirror responses to the first. Rather than two ends of the same spectrum, some reporters interpreted the paragraphs as describing two distinct types of behavior. These reporters explicitly explained that their mayoral candidates were adept at maintaining both cosmopolitan and provincial networks, so both paragraphs very accurately described them. As a result, more reporters found the second paragraph to be a good description of their mayoral candidate. For most candidates, however, a high score on the cosmopolitan measure resulted in a low score on the provincial measure.

EVEN PROVINCIAL MAYORAL CANDIDATES INNOVATE Further evidence that the two questions successfully measured the presence and absence of cosmopolitan networks is their nearly identical relationships to campaign sophistication. Both attributes are at best only weakly related to the sophistication of mayoral candidates' campaigns. Of the candidates who were fairly or very cosmopolitan, 77 percent relied on two or more sophisticated tactics in their campaigns. So did 63 percent of those who were only slightly or somewhat cosmopolitan. Similarly, of the candidates who were only slightly or somewhat provincial, 75 percent relied on two or more sophisticated tactics—but so did 67 percent of those who were fairly or very provincial.

A stronger relationship might have been discovered if candidates' behavior was either directly observed or self-reported. Yet a weak relationship probably exists because political candidates are different from potential adopters of other types of innovations. As aspiring political elites, those seeking public office are already more cosmopolitan than the general public. Perhaps any influence to be gained from interactions with associates has reached a threshold by the time people make a decision to run for public office. While diversity in mayoral candidates' level of cosmopolitanness is present, these findings suggest that further expanding their network of associates has an existing, but very limited, relationship to their receptiveness toward new campaign strategies.

Do Political Consultants Promote Adoption?

A second personal characteristic of most innovators is frequent contact with change agents. Change agents are professionals external to the local social system who work to influence whether and how new technologies are adopted. Typically, change agents represent either a nonprofit organization or a government agency with an interest in promoting the use of an innovation. They initiate contact with potential innovators and help them become aware of the need to alter their behavior. They do so by pointing out why existing alternatives are not working as well as the benefits to be gained from change.[21] In short, they provide information that can alter existing schemata.

It is possible that political consultants—although promoting their own material interests, rather than those of a change-oriented agency—are fulfilling a change-agent role in the diffusion of new campaign technologies to candidates in smaller electoral districts. As noted, the number of consultants working in the United States has risen dramatically.[22] Consultants seeking work in a more competitive market might be responsible for creating a demand for their services among candidates in local governments to provide themselves with a new source of clients.

Working on national and statewide races is considered a sign of prestige within the profession. Consultants capable of earning a living by working solely on races with national or statewide constituencies are not likely to work in local political arenas. Yet the number of these prestigious races cannot provide full-time employment for all the people working as professional political consultants in the United States. The fact that local government elections are often held in odd-numbered years may also increase their appeal to political consultants struggling to make ends meet. With a client base of local government candidates, consultants who cannot afford downtime between national or state election cycles are guaranteed a consistent source of employment. Many general political consultants perceive themselves as local government candidates' source of information about innovative communication approaches. This sentiment was expressed by one consultant, who wrote, "It's my job to stay up-to-date on the latest techniques available and then determine . . . how best to use them." Consequently, political consultants may be altering local government candidates' campaign schema by contacting them to promote their services and the benefits of new-style campaign strategies.

Contact with Political Consultants Encourages Sophistication

Questions on the mail survey to general political consultants were included in order to probe the relationship between consultants and their clientele. Several were asked to determine whether general consultants actively recruit clients running for local public offices. For example, general consultants who had worked with local government candidates in the past two election cycles were asked to identify the number of new local clients with whom they had initiated contact, as well as the number of new local clients who had sought out their services. Any inclination to underestimate their efforts to cultivate a local client base should have been ameliorated by the assurance of anonymity. Responses reveal, however, that the majority of general consultants is not aggressively creating a demand for their services. Sixty-three percent indicated that they initiated contact with none of their local clients. Another 20 percent did so with less than one-half of their new local clients. A smaller number of consultants appeared to be making an effort to reach out to candidates in local electoral districts. Fourteen percent, for example, made the first attempt to establish a relationship with more than one-half of their clients who ran for local government offices. Only 3 percent initiated contact with all of their local clients.

Political consultants' activities do not mirror those of a traditional change agent, who typically promotes the use of a new technology to as many people as possible because its use is perceived as beneficial. Since consultants are driven by a profit motive, those able to attract enough clients to make a living will not initiate additional contacts, even if many candidates have not yet adopted new-style campaigns. Consultants also may not encourage the diffusion of communication technology to preserve their own candidates' technological advantage over opponents. Thus, the smaller percentage of consultants initiating contact probably works for less-successful firms struggling to build up a client base. Despite this discovery of the passivity of the majority of general consultants, however, making an effort to more fully understand why local candidates seek out professional help highlights the importance of direct and indirect contact with campaign professionals.

Consultants sought out by their local government clients were provided with a list of factors that may have prompted these clients to initiate contact and were asked to identify the two most important ones. Although most general consultants are not actively targeting local candidates, indirect and direct contact with campaign professionals still influences local government candidates' decisions. Only a small fraction of the general consultants, 3 percent and 1 percent, respectively, believed that their efforts to promote services through advertising or speaking engagements attracted their clients. Yet indirectly learning about a consultant through a prior client was by far the most frequently selected factor, at 88 percent. In addition, direct interaction with other campaign professionals who made referrals was selected by 44 percent of the respondents, making it the second-most common influence on clients' choices. Although selected by fewer consultants, 29 percent and 28 percent, respectively, indirect contact through the references of party officials and media coverage of prior races were still perceived as affecting candidates' hiring decisions. Campaign professionals do not act like traditional change agents, but their activity in local political arenas appears to have a similar effect. At least some of the candidates who come into contact with them, either directly or indirectly, appear to learn about the potential benefits to be gained from purchasing professional services.

Finally, the smaller number of general consultants who initiated contact with their local government clients were provided with a list of potential methods for doing so and asked to identify the two most important ones. Again, very few saw broad promotional efforts as effective ways to cultivate clientele. Only 3 percent chose speaking engagements and 7 percent advertising efforts. Personal efforts were perceived to be far more effective, with 86 percent of these consultants selecting telephone calls, 48 percent selecting face-to-face meetings, and 36 percent selecting letters. Hence, consultants actively trying to recruit local candidates might call or write to those whom they suspect might want to purchase professional services. More informally, they might make a point of introducing themselves to potential clients at political events.

Regardless of whether candidates sought out professional assistance or were actively persuaded by consultants, the act of hiring a general consultant signaled their receptiveness to new campaign tactics. The general consultants were asked to identify how many of their local clients with past campaign experience relied on a new campaign tactic. Seventy-six percent of the consultants indicated that at least some of their experienced local clients had adopted a new tactic. This high percentage suggests that contact with campaign professionals, whether accomplished purposefully or by coincidence, appears to affect local government candidates' strategic decisions.

As a result, one would expect the campaign sophistication of mayoral candidates in midsized cities to be related to their contact with political consultants. To measure this type of contact, reporters were asked the following question:

> I'd like to know your estimate of how much contact these candidates had with campaign professionals before this election. So, prior to the most recent election, how often would you estimate that these candidates' professional and social activities brought them into contact with professional political consultants (such as managers, pollster, media specialists, etc.)?

Note that the term *contact* in this paragraph was clarified, as reporters were told that it included any type of interaction with campaign professionals. This clarification was necessary because limiting the definition of *contact* to previously hiring professionals would prevent reporters from describing first-time candidates. According to reporters, 37 percent of mayoral candidates almost never had contact with professionals, and for 21 percent such contact was rare. Twenty-five percent had occasional contact with professionals, and for 17 percent such contact was frequent.

In addition, the frequency of contact with campaign professionals is related to mayoral candidates' campaign sophistication. Eighty-three percent of the candidates who had occasional or frequent contact with political consultants used two or more sophisticated tactics, while only 57 percent of those who almost never or rarely had such contact did likewise.

CONSULTANTS' PRESENCE PRODUCES A PROGRESSIVE TREND

Together, these findings suggest that the trend toward new-style local campaigns will continue to expand. When campaign professionals enter a local electoral arena, they inevitably come into both direct and indirect contact with other potential adopters. Simply by working for some candidates in smaller electoral districts, they familiarize others with their services. Even if political consultants have not consciously adopted the role of change agents, their activities produce similar results. As this trend has already been established, the increasing influence of their presence in local electoral politics would be difficult, if not impossible, to stem.

The Influence of Candidate Audiences

Candidates' need to persuade others provides further insight into their decision to go sophisticated. In other diffusion scenarios, people are free to rely on their own evaluations of new technology when deciding whether to innovate. In fact, "as the first to adopt a new idea in their system, they cannot depend upon the subjective evaluations of the innovation from other members of their system."[23] Political candidates, on the other hand, cannot afford to ignore the way members of their social system will evaluate their adoption of new-style campaign tactics. Their success depends on persuading other members of their social system to support them. In particular, candidates must be concerned with evaluations by reporters, who control the type of media coverage a campaign receives, as well as by voters, who ultimately decide whether a candidate will succeed or fail. If candidates suspect that voters and reporters in their local political arenas expect sophisticated tactics, they will probably be more receptive to information about such innovations and will adjust their local campaign schema to include new-style campaign strategies.

Campaign Strategies Are Used to Evaluate Candidates

Interviews with political reporters strongly suggest that such expectations play a role in candidates' campaign strategies. When asked whether they thought citizens in their municipalities expected mayoral candidates to use any particular tactics, nearly all (95 percent) responded affirmatively. Those who said yes were then asked to identify the specific tactics they perceived as expected. This query was left open-ended, without asking reporters to evaluate a list of all available tactics. Without this prompting, reporters may have overlooked some activities. Yet responses to the question still serve as a general indicator of which tactics were most expected. The expected tactics, listed in order from the most to the least expected, are speeches (71 percent), yard signs (67 percent), canvassing (49 percent), newspaper ads (37 percent), radio ads (35 percent), direct mail (28 percent), television ads (22 percent), literature drops (21 percent), fundraising events (15 percent), phone banks (7 percent), public opinion polls (3 percent), and Internet sites (1 percent).

Discovering that the four most expected tactics are traditional should not come as a surprise, given their frequent appearance in local campaigns. These four tactics—speeches, yard signs, canvassing, and newspaper ads—are followed by direct mail and radio advertisements, which are also commonly used in local campaigns because they enable candidates to target small groups of voters. Television advertisements and literature drops were both mentioned by slightly more than 20 percent of the reporters. (Some reporters may have forgotten to mention literature drops because they are so similar to canvassing.) Fewer reporters identified fundraising events or telephone banks. The least expected tactics were public opinion polls and Internet sites. Public opinion polls probably do not become expected tactics because their use is often not visible to the general public. Candidates use them to gather information from voters, not to send messages to them. The only time that citizens, as well as reporters, learn whether a candidate relied on a poll is if the results are released to the press. Finally, Internet sites were probably mentioned rarely because their use in local campaigns was still a novelty at the time the interviews were completed.

In addition to merely identifying expected tactics, several reporters took the initiative to speculate about the consequences a candidate would face for not using them. They explained that the failure to use an expected tactic would hurt a candidate's chances of winning. In a city where television commercials were expected, for example, one reporter said that people would think that a candidate without them had a weak campaign. Another reporter predicted people's reaction to the absence of yard signs in a city where they were expected. He said that it would be perceived as an indicator of limited public support because others would assume that candidates who failed to use yard signs had trouble persuading people to post their signs. He concluded that the notion that these candidates simply decided to spend their money on other tactics would not occur to voters in his city.

While reporters were attributing these reactions to the voting public, their own standards of evaluating candidates may also be represented in their responses. Determining whether candidates lived up to the ideal campaigns of reporters in their communities suggests that reporters use expectations to evaluate campaigns in a similar way.

For example, 152 mayoral candidates used anywhere from one to four more sophisticated tactics than were expected in their municipalities; 71 percent of these candidates were described as running in a serious race. For 37 candidates, no difference existed between the number of sophisticated tactics expected and used; 54 percent of these candidates were described as running in serious races. Finally, 15 candidates used one or two fewer sophisticated tactics than expected in their electoral districts. Only 4 (27 percent) of these candidates were described as running in serious races. The pattern of reporters' responses indicates that voters are not the only ones who use their expectations to identify viable candidates. Candidates who want to be taken seriously by these primary audiences should attempt to meet their expectations.

Candidates Respond to Audience Expectations

In fact, mayoral candidates do appear to alter their campaign strategies to meet expectations. With the exception of political polls, a relationship exists between expectations and the use of sophisticated tactics in their campaigns. The second column in table 3.2 lists the difference in the percentage of candidates using each key sophisticated tactic when these are expected, as opposed to when they are unexpected. A negative relationship exists between an expectation for public opinion polls and their use. While 33 percent of the mayoral candidates used polls when these were expected, 41 percent used polls when these were not identified as an expected tactic. This pattern may have emerged because the limited visibility of polling precludes the development of the public's expectation for them. Yet candidates rely on polls anyway because polls help them use other tactics more effectively. For the remainder of the sophisticated tactics, however, expectations are positively related to use. Ten percent more of the candidates running in cities where targeted direct mail was expected relied on the tactic. This pattern becomes more extreme for radio and television advertisements. Radio commercials were relied on by 42 percent more of the candidates in electoral districts where they were expected. For television commercials, the percentage increase was 53 percent.

Clearly, candidates respond to community expectations in developing their campaign strategies. Yet establishing the existence of this relationship does not explain why these expectations developed in the first place. Further exploration of their origins is warranted. Consequently, characteristics that may encourage the development of such expectations are covered next.

Does the Electorate's Socioeconomic Status Affect Expectations?

When local constituents have a high socioeconomic status, local candidates may believe that they need to use sophisticated tactics in order to live up to

Table 3.2   Expectations and Past Campaigns Affect Use of Sophisticated Tactics

Tactic	Difference in Use When Expected	Difference in Use with Frequent Past Use
Public Opinion Polls	−8	+57
Television Advertisements	+53	+63
Targeted Direct Mail	+10	+26
Radio Advertisements	+42	+19

Source: 1998 interviews about the most recent mayoral candidates in midsized cities.

voters' expectations. Higher socioeconomic status encompasses higher levels of education and more professional occupations. Both types of achievements often bring people into contact with either communication technology itself or with information about communication technology. People with higher socioeconomic status are also more likely to have cosmopolitan networks of associates experienced with new technological innovations. When people know about alternative methods of communication provided by technology, they may wonder why local government candidates have not adopted these.

As with candidates, voters' general awareness of technology through the mass media or other sources is less likely to affect their expectations than are personal experiences. The Internet provides a good example. After all of the media coverage of the Internet as the "information superhighway" of the future, most members of the general public, regardless of their socioeconomic status, are aware that it exists. Yet people who do not own a computer or use one at work are not likely to have "surfed the Web." People with higher socioeconomic status are more apt to have had such experiences and thus to wonder whether a candidate has a website. It probably takes only a few voter requests for a Web address to make a candidate think he or she needs a Web page on the Internet. Sophisticated voters may expect their candidates to mirror their own technological proficiency. As a result, new-style campaigns may occur more frequently in smaller electoral districts where residents have a higher socioeconomic status.

CANDIDATES INNOVATE, REGARDLESS OF VOTERS' STATUS   Measures of socioeconomic status often incorporate levels of both income and educational achievement. Data from the 1990 Census of Populations were used to measure these two aspects of socioeconomic status in the 109 municipalities where mayoral campaigns were studied.[24] The income level of each electorate was represented by the per capita income of each city, which ranged from $7,276 to $27,092, with an average of $13,370. Yet variation in income levels was unrelated to the sophistication of political campaigns. Candidates used similar numbers of sophisticated tactics, regardless of their constituents' financial standing. The wealth of the electorate appears to be unrelated to the campaign styles preferred by political candidates. Meanwhile, educational achievement was represented by the percentage of the population in each city with college degrees. Educational achievement also varied considerably. The percentage of college graduates ranged from only 6 percent to 47.9 percent, with an average of 19.2 percent. Unlike income levels, educational achievement appears to be weakly related to campaign sophistication. For example, in cities where fewer than 20 percent of the population graduated from college, 36 percent of the candidates used more than two sophisticated tactics, and where the percentage of college graduates ranged from 21 percent to 40 percent, the number of candidates with comparable sophistication levels only jumped to 47 percent. The data do suggest that extremely high education levels may be linked to campaign sophistication because in the two cities where the percentage of college graduates exceeded 40 percent, all four mayoral candidates relied on all available sophisticated tactics. Yet this subtle pattern provides little insight into candidates' strategic decisions.

Do Past Electoral Campaigns Shape Expectations?

Another possible influence on expectations for future local campaigns is the types of campaigns occurring in a city's past. Local candidates are not the only ones with a schema of local campaigns for office. Other actors in the political arena, such as voters and reporters, also rely on schema based on their experiences to process information about local political activity. Recall that each schema includes a conception of a general pattern, as well as only a limited number of illustrative examples.[25] After several new-style campaigns in a local political arena have occurred, these may become the repertoire of examples people use to refer to local campaigns. At this point, sophisticated communication tactics would become expected. This phenomenon is described as the diffusion effect. As more members of a social system adopt a particular innovation, the pressure increases for others to adopt it. Early innovators may be asked to explain why they adopted an innovation, but late adopters will be asked why they have not.[26]

At least by the point of widespread adoption, local political reporters may even begin to evaluate candidates' chances for success based on their campaign strategies. Reporters covering congressional races often use criteria such as fundraising ability, standing in the polls, and backing of political insiders to determine whether challengers have a chance to win. Those perceived as losers, largely because they cannot raise enough money to run new-style campaigns, are simply not covered.[27] "Many times, their [congressional candidates'] campaigns are written off before they have begun, and even when candidates are awarded some coverage, it is usually to note that they will not win."[28] After becoming accustomed to seeing new-style campaigns in their local political arenas, political reporters probably develop similar criteria for evaluating local candidates.

For example, Mayor Jerry Jennings's 1997 re-election efforts appear to have created new expectations for local government candidates in Albany. In 1998, the local newspaper reported that candidates believe they need to raise unprecedented amounts of money in order to run for city and county offices.[29] One politician noted, "The Jennings campaign—particularly its heavy use of television spots—set a new standard of performance for candidates and expectations from the electorate about how a race should look."[30]

Reporters questioned Jennings about his decision to incorporate sophisticated tactics into his campaign. It seems that future local candidates who do not follow in his footsteps might be asked why they have not. Hence, candidates probably will continue to use new-style campaigns in localities where these have been used in the past.

Past Campaigns Influence Both Reporters and Voters

Reporters' opinions signal that such a process occurs. After the discussion of expected tactics, reporters were simply asked to explain why they thought voters anticipated certain activities but not others. Most of the responses to this open-ended query can be quickly summarized with one word—tradition. Seventy-three percent of the reporters explained that voters' current expectations were based on the types of mayoral campaigns witnessed in the past. Voters, according to reporters, became accustomed to seeing the tactics that candidates chose to use. Interestingly, other types of explanations were offered only when expectations were restricted to traditional activities. For example, 16 percent of the reporters indicated that the electorate expected grassroots tactics because they wanted direct, personal contact with their future public officials. Another 7 percent said that the small size of the electorate made people realize that more sophisticated tactics were unnecessary. Finally, 4 percent claimed that even though their local governments' electoral districts had recently experienced population growth, citizens maintained a "small town attitude" about the types of tactics appropriate in municipal political campaigns. Yet wherever sophisticated campaigns had taken root, reporters abandoned such explanations and indicated that past campaigns shaped expectations.

To further explore the impact of past political campaigns, reporters were also asked to estimate the use of specific tactics in their respective city's three previous mayoral races. Some newly hired reporters were unfamiliar with past mayoral campaigns and were unable to provide such information. However, data on past campaigns were collected on 70 percent of the 109 cities included in the study. The percentage of cities where previous mayoral candidates relied on specific tactics either frequently or almost always, listed in order of the most- to the least-used tactic, is yard signs (100 percent), speeches (97 percent), literature drops (95 percent), fundraising events (92 percent), newspaper ads (83 percent), canvassing (83 percent), direct mail (77 percent), phone banks (66 percent), radio ads (57 percent), polls (41 percent), television ads (31 percent), and Internet sites (0 percent). The list should look familiar. With minor exceptions, it mirrors the description of recent mayoral candidates' use of specific tactics presented in chapter 2. (The minor exceptions are the transposed positions of speeches and yard signs, as well as those of television advertisements and public opinion polls.) This similarity suggests that a connection exists between past and current use.

The patterns presented in the third column of table 3.2 provide further evidence of such a connection. It lists the increase in the percentage of recent mayoral candidates using each key sophisticated tactic when it had been used frequently in past campaigns. Clearly, when prior mayoral candidates used sophisticated tactics, the most recent candidates in the same cities were more apt to have relied on them as well. In cities where radio was a common tactic, 19 percent more of recent mayoral candidates used it. For direct mail, the percentage increase was 26 percent. The patterns for the two most complex tactics are even more dramatic. Past use of public opinion polls results in 57 percent more current candidates polling, while the percentage of increase related to the past use of television is 63 percent.

COMMUNITY EXPECTATIONS PRODUCE AN IRREVERSIBLE TREND   One consequence of this strong relationship is that the trend toward new-style campaigns in smaller electoral districts is not likely to be reversed. After communication technology has been used by winning candidates, people attempting to replicate their results in future races will imitate their efforts. These strategic decisions may be driven by candidates' own evaluations and by the altered expectations of voters and reporters. Once sophisticated tactics have become expected in a particular electoral arena, their presence is used to estimate the quality of candidates' campaigns. At this point, very few candidates would limit themselves to traditional activities by choice. Although grassroots tactics are an adequate (and, arguably, superior) method for communicating with smaller constituencies, they come to be perceived as insufficient. Thus, it seems that new-style campaigns in local politics are here to stay.

The Influence of the Political Environment

As the preceding account indicates, some personal experiences that increase candidates' knowledge about sophisticated campaign tactics, as well as about their evaluations of constituency expectations, are related to the adoption of new-style campaign strategies. Yet information about an innovation does not guarantee its adoption. Rather, "individuals generally tend to expose themselves to ideas that are in accordance with their interests, needs or existing attitudes."[31] People are less receptive to, and might not even notice, information about innovations unless current practices are not meeting their expectations or fulfilling their desires. When this type of frustration exists, people may even seek out innovations corresponding to their perceived needs.[32] Aside from a few candidates who run on a lark, candidates typically run for office with a strong desire to win. Whenever their electoral success is uncertain, candidates are more likely to be receptive to new campaign tactics that could improve their chances of winning. Thus, the presence of new-style campaigns at the local level should also be related to elements of the political environment affecting candidates' chances for electoral success.

Does Competition Affect Campaign Strategies?

The most obvious of such elements is the existence of a competitive race. Candidates running for safe seats have no incentive to expend the resources necessary to incorporate sophisticated tactics. For political consultants to be hired, "the election must be contested and not one-sided, so that a candidate is motivated to enlist help."[33] When re-election is guaranteed, candidates often fail to undertake even traditional grassroots activities, let alone the expensive, sophisticated tactics of new-style campaigns. Such an example, once again drawn from Albany, New York, illustrates this interplay between competitive races and campaign activities.

Competition and Innovation in Albany, New York

Until recently, the city of Albany was controlled by a Democratic political machine with influence comparable to, if not surpassing, the Daly machine in Chicago. As the machine's preferred mayoral candidate, Erastus Corning achieved the distinction of the longest-serving mayor in U.S. history by holding office for forty-two years. He was first elected in 1941 and served until his death in 1983. A recent biographer describes most of Corning's mayoral elections as "a blur of landslides" and notes that "few gave Corning even the slightest scare."[34]

As a result, he rarely undertook any activities to guarantee his re-election, and this passivity nearly cost him his office in 1973. Corning underestimated a challenge from local businessman Carl Touhey, who accepted the Republican nomination. While Touhey was literally wearing holes in his shoes, campaigning door-to-door and spending nearly $70,000 of his own money, Corning remained confident and inactive.[35] During interviews with reporters, he insisted that the responsibilities of his job left no time to campaign door-to-door and suggested that a walking tour of the city would be a waste of his time.[36] When asked about the race, he confided, "No, I'm not worried about the election. If I did, I would have worried myself to death many years ago."[37] Yet when Touhey released a public opinion poll showing that he had a slight lead over the mayor, Corning changed his tune and said, "I'm running scared."[38] Soon afterward, he campaigned door-to-door "for the first time in recent memory."[39] Despite these last-minute efforts, Corning's campaign efforts were minimal. According to an account in the local newspaper one week before the election, he had no campaign headquarters, no campaign literature, and no campaign streamers or placards. In addition, Corning had purchased no newspaper, radio, or television advertisements. In fact, Corning claimed that he had not "raised or spent a penny on his campaign for re-election" and did not expect to spend any.[40]

Corning narrowly won re-election by 3,556 votes—and undocumented claims still persist that the machine stole votes to provide Corning with a win in 1973.[41] According to one account, the near loss

> served as a wake-up call to Corning and his machine cronies that the old complacency would no longer carry the day. Losing, once incomprehensible, was suddenly in the realm of possibility for the mayor with the historic tenure. Re-election had gone from being a formality to something Corning would have to earn.[42]

When Corning faced an unprecedented challenge in the Democratic primary four years later, he took the threat more seriously. Although he relied extensively on Democratic committee members to canvass their neighbors, Corning delayed surgery to replace a painfully deteriorated hip joint in order to campaign in person throughout the race.[43] He also spent $51,000 on the primary race, with approximately $16,500 of that amount dedicated to the purchase of television airtime. Apparently, most of the television expenses were funded by a $15,000 personal loan from Corning during the closing days of the campaign.[44] In consequence, within the time frame of one election cycle, electoral insecurity drove Corning from undertaking almost no campaign activities to spending his own money on television commercials.

Competition Is Linked to Campaign Sophistication

To explore the effects of competition in midsized cities, reporters were first questioned about whether the most recent mayoral race in their city was contested. Those answering affirmatively were asked to elaborate on the quality of competition by explaining whether the race's outcome was a foregone conclusion or an uncertainty. Reporters' responses signal the health of democracy in America's municipalities. Incumbents ran unopposed in only 8 percent of the 109 midsized cities. Races were only formally contested in 31 percent of the cities, but in 61 percent races were seriously contested. Voters in most cities were offered a choice between at least two viable candidates for mayor on election day.

However, those who find the trend toward sophisticated local campaigns disturbing may be disappointed to find that it is linked to serious competition. Only 33 percent of unchallenged incumbents used two or more sophisticated tactics. For candidates in only formally contested races, this percentage increases to 50 percent. Yet 81 percent of the candidates engaged in serious competition relied on at least two sophisticated tactics.

HEALTHY COMPETITION TRIGGERS INNOVATION   Competition is essential to the health of democracy. Challengers force incumbents to defend their positions and provide citizens with a way to hold public officials accountable for past decisions. Yet as long as competition creates electoral insecurity, candidates will be tempted to innovate in order to improve their chances for success. Although the adoption of sophisticated campaigns may have other negative consequences, these are probably first adopted when a governing system is functioning optimally. During times when candidates are insecure, they will be more apt to adopt new tactics that promise an improved ability to contact and persuade voters.

Does Political Culture Suppress New-Style Campaigning?

Other elements of the local political environments may affect whether candidates' feelings of electoral uncertainty will be assuaged by traditional old-style campaign activities. Political culture, for example, could affect candidates' willingness to accept new-style campaigns. Three political cultures, which developed in different geographic areas as a result of migration patterns, have been identified in the United States. In each political culture, residents have different expectations about appropriate government activities, the types of people who should be involved in politics, and the way the art of government should be practiced.[45]

Regions of the country characterized by a "moralistic culture" are of particular interest. This culture emphasizes commitment to the public interest and honesty in government. Moreover, everyone is expected to participate in politics.[46] In places where the moralistic culture is dominant, "there is considerably more amateur participation in politics."[47] New-style campaigns, with their emphasis on sophisticated tactics and professional expertise, are the antithesis of amateur politics. Therefore, new-style campaigns may be less prevalent in Maine, Vermont, Michigan, Wisconsin, Minnesota, North Dakota, Colorado, Utah, and Oregon, which are the states identified with a dominant moralistic culture.

Candidates for School Board Go Sophisticated in Madison, Wisconsin

The infiltration of new-style campaigns into moralistic states is illustrated by a 1997 school board race in Madison, Wisconsin, population 208,054, between incumbent Deborah Lawson and challenger Tom Ragatz. Ragatz, a lawyer and certified public accountant, entered the race because he was dissatisfied with the school board's fiscal management. He turned to new-style campaigning because canvassing door-to-door was too time-consuming, whereas communication technology provides "more bang for your effort."[48] With extensive political contacts, he relied on the assistance of unpaid volunteers and advisers, rather than hiring a campaign manager. Although his campaign included literature drops, public announcements, and canvassing, Ragatz also spent more than $40,000 on technical assistance from a public relations firm, broadcast television spots, radio ads, and targeted direct mail.[49]

Lawson, who won the race with 54 percent of the vote, claimed that she felt pressure to respond with similar tactics.[50] "If I could have gotten away without it [sophisticated tactics], I would have," she said. Her comments imply that competitive contests can become an arms race. She spent about $25,000 to supplement a traditional grassroots approach. Her efforts included television spots, radio ads, and direct mail targeted with the assistance of a list broker. She was able to hold down her expenses because her sister, who has since run county and state campaigns, served as her campaign manager, and her husband had a background in advertising.[51]

After the election, Michael Jacob, outreach director for the Wisconsin Democracy Campaign, complained, "A proud tradition is at risk. . . . When big money starts to come into school board races, it usually means that it will just get worse."[52] Lawson pointed out that no Madison school board candidates have turned to television since her 1997 race, but suspects that it will return in competitive races. "When there is any sort of issue at all, local races are ratcheting up," she said.[53]

POLITICAL CULTURE FAILS TO HINDER SOPHISTICATED EFFORTS Additional evidence indicates that political culture is unrelated to the phenomenon of new-style local campaigns. Of the 217 mayoral candidates, 19 percent ran in states with moralistic political cultures. These states were Michigan, Minnesota, North Dakota, Oregon, Utah, and Wisconsin. With the exception of Minnesota, where only one city was studied, some candidates in each one of these states relied on none of the sophisticated tactics available to them. Yet with the exceptions of Oregon and North Dakota, there were also candidates in each of these states who used all four sophisticated tactics. (Again, only one city was studied in each of these two states.) Moreover, the percentage of candidates relying on new-style campaigns in moralistic states was nearly identical to that of those running elsewhere. In states with a moralistic political culture, 68 percent of the mayoral candidates relied on two or more sophisticated tactics. Meanwhile, 69 percent of the candidates in other types of states followed suit.

State political cultures are possibly less distinct now than at the time they were first identified. The nationalizing force of the news media and of swift communication technology broadens citizens' horizons and may homogenize regional political cultures. Even if this scenario is accurate, it is clear that new-style campaigns have made inroads in places like Madison, Wisconsin, where amateurism was at least once heralded as the appropriate form of participation in government.

Does the Structure of Local Party Organizations Affect Campaign Styles?

Another element of the local political environment potentially affecting whether electoral insecurity drives candidates toward sophisticated tactics is the existence and/or activities of a local party organization. The structure of party organizations can affect the types of campaigns that candidates choose to run when races are competitive.[54] When local parties offer support that reduces the threat of electoral insecurity, local candidates should feel more comfortable maintaining a traditional campaign style. Yet in communities with nonpartisan elections or unorganized party systems, the lack of assistance may enhance candidates' feelings of insecurity and may encourage them to turn to the reassurances of professional expertise and communication technology.

The Effect of Electoral Insecurity in Visalia, California

The political experiences of Visalia, California (population 91,565), mayor Don Landers reveals how insecurity can lead candidates to hire political consultants, even when they do not feel pressured to incorporate sophisticated communication technology. Landers lost two bids for a seat on City Council in 1989 and 1991, after coordinating his own grassroots campaign efforts. He remained active in city politics and was appointed to an open seat on the Council in 1995. When his 1997 re-election rolled around, Landers did not want to risk losing, so he "pulled out all the stops" by hiring a local political consultant. For $3,500, the consultant designed an effective logo, wrote the campaign flier, organized volunteer literature drops, facilitated weekly meetings, and provided advice throughout the campaign. Overall, Landers spent about $13,500 to hold on to his seat. Landers was up for re-election again in 2001, but decided against hiring professional expertise. Since 1997, he was selected by fellow council members to serve as mayor. Along with the position comes widespread name recognition. Yet Landers revealed his biggest reason for not hiring professional assistance—with a winning campaign under his belt, he now feels comfortable making strategic decisions on his own.[55]

Types of Support Provided by Parties

In the not-so-distant past, local party organizations in many regions of the country were often either nonexistent or in a state of disarray. Examples of such parties included Republican organizations in the solidly Democratic South and minority parties in cities controlled by political machines. Furthermore, numerous U.S. local governments (as well as the state of Nebraska) have adopted nonpartisan elections. This reform denies parties a formal role in the nomination of candidates for office and excludes references to candidates' party affiliations on election ballots. Thus, nonpartisan elections deprive local parties of their primary function and discourage their involvement in local politics. The absence of a well-organized party, which characterizes some U.S. local governments, may increase candidates' sense of electoral insecurity by limiting their access to the resources of volunteers and grassroots expertise. Without a base of party activists, candidates may fear that they cannot attract enough volunteers on their own to successfully carry out the traditional activities associated with old-style campaigns. In addition, novice candidates, unable to seek advice from party officials with campaign experience, may not trust their abilities to organize a grassroots campaign even if volunteers are available.

Where party organizations are present, however, research has found that national and state party committees, as well as county and municipal party committees, are becoming institutionalized. In short, they are acquiring the trappings of organizational permanence and are providing more consistent assistance to candidates, including distributing literature, arranging campaign events, fundraising, attracting media coverage, and organizing registration drives.[56] This type of support from a local party organization could reduce local candidates' uncertainties and their need to innovate. Even those facing serious opponents would have access to the volunteer resources that are essential to a successful old-style campaign. In fact, the existence of serious competition surely enhances party volunteers' willingness to perform such activities. If they believed that their participation might make the difference between winning and losing, potential volunteers would be more willing to donate their time to the campaign effort. Meanwhile, experienced party activists could explain how such activities were used successfully in past campaigns. Consequently, local party organization with the ability to provide traditional campaign services may be related to fewer new-style campaigns in local political arenas.

Local party organizations, however, are not necessarily limited to providing only traditional campaign services to their local candidates. Campaign services provided by national and state party committees have been extended to include assistance with the sophisticated tactics of new-style campaigns. National and state party committees often provide assistance by conducting public opinion polls, by purchasing strategic advice from political consultants, or even by producing television and radio ads.[57] Although local party committees have less ability to raise the money needed to provide such services, some may be attempting to follow the examples set by state and national committees. In places where local party organizations provide assistance with sophisticated tactics or contribute the financial support needed to purchase them, local candidates may be more apt to rely on them.

Limited Effects of Support from Parties

Of 109 cities studied, only 33 percent hold partisan elections. This pattern is not surprising, as the adoption of nonpartisanship has been widespread among America's local governments. Unexpectedly, however, more of the candidates running in these partisan cities relied on sophisticated tactics than did their counterparts in nonpartisan cities. Eighty-three percent of the candidates running in partisan races relied on two or more sophisticated tactics, while only 62 percent of those in nonpartisan races matched this level of sophistication.

This unexpected finding can be at least partially attributed to the decreased chances of competition under nonpartisanship. Most nonpartisan cities lack an organization dedicated to the recruitment of challengers. For this reason, and because voters rely more heavily on incumbency as a voting cue when partisan cues are absent, incumbents face less serious challenges in nonpartisan elections.[58] Finally, partisan cities are found somewhat more often in states characterized by competitive two-party systems, and this competition may filter into local political arenas.[59] The nonpartisan cities included in the study were less likely to have had a competitive race. Mayoral elections were uncontested in 11 percent of nonpartisan cities, but in only 3 percent of partisan cities. In addition, only 58 percent of races in nonpartisan cities were described as seriously contested, but 67 percent of the elections in partisan cities fell into this category. Any remaining relationship between partisanship and sophisticated campaigns may simply be the result of expectations generated by a history of more competitive races.

Within the smaller number of partisan cities, however, when parties are institutionalized and provide assistance with traditional tactics, candidates may believe that their volunteer base and grassroots activities will be sufficient even in competitive races. Reporters were asked two questions to gauge whether parties were a resource of advice and assistance in the use of grassroots activities. First, reporters were asked whether the local Democratic and Republican Parties had a permanent headquarters, allowing prospective candidates to more easily locate party officials and know where to turn for advice. Of the partisan mayoral candidates, 31 percent ran in cities where their parties had established a permanent headquarters. Yet this resource made little difference in the sophistication of their campaigns. Eight-six percent of the candidates with a party headquarters relied on two or more sophisticated tactics, as did 82 percent of those lacking this resource.

Second, reporters were asked whether the local Democratic and Republican Parties organized volunteers on behalf of their candidates. With such assistance, candidates could feel more secure about their abilities to undertake traditional tactics. Only four mayoral candidates (6 percent) could not rely on such assistance from their respective parties. Of these four candidates, one relied on two sophisticated tactics, while three relied on three. Yet of all the candidates who did receive such assistance from their parties, most relied on two or more sophisticated tactics. In other words, traditional party assistance did not suppress their desire to adopt new tactics. For example, 28 percent relied on all four sophisticated tactics, 25 percent relied on three, and 29 percent relied on two. The activities of local parties could be plumbed in order to more accurately measure the level of support they provide to candidates. Yet at first glance, party assistance with traditional activities appears unrelated to candidates' strategic decisions. Given the movement toward candidate-centered campaigns at all other levels of American politics, perhaps this finding should come as no surprise. Although candidates accept help with grassroots activities, this assistance does not diminish the number of candidates succumbing to the lure of sophisticated tactics.

More surprising, however, is that even the provision of assistance with sophisticated tactics had no impact on candidates' campaign styles. This type of assistance was also measured by two questions in the telephone interviews. With one question, reporters were asked whether the parties in their cities provided candidates with professional campaign services and advice. This type of assistance was provided to 36 percent of the partisan mayoral candidates. The relationship between such assistance and campaign strategy is nonexistent, as identical percentages of those receiving and not receiving such assistance relied on two or more sophisticated tactics.

Reporters were also asked whether the political parties in their cities made substantial financial contributions to candidates. Although local party officials may not have the necessary infrastructure to perform professional services, they can contribute to sophistication by providing financial assistance. Thirty-three percent of the partisan mayoral candidates received this type of financial assistance. This assistance was shown to have a somewhat stronger relationship to candidates' campaign strategies. While 91 percent of those receiving financial assistance relied on two or more sophisticated tactics, 78 percent of those without it followed suit. It is important to remember, however, that most municipalities have nonpartisan elections. So even though financial support from political parties helps candidates afford new-style campaigns, it will not affect most local candidates' strategic decisions.

LOCAL CAMPAIGNS ARE CANDIDATE-CENTERED   These patterns
suggest that factors other than party assistance are largely responsible for candidates' decisions to adopt the trappings of new-style campaigns. When parties offer such assistance, it is accepted, and financial contributions appear at
least somewhat linked to candidates' abilities to incorporate the trappings of
new-style campaigns. However, many candidates lacking the aid of their
respective political parties, either because it is not provided or because elections are nonpartisan, find other ways to incorporate communication technology into their campaign strategies. This type of autonomy reflects the
development of candidate-centered campaigns that is well documented in
America's state and national elections.

Conclusion

Comparing the campaigns of these mayoral candidates has revealed three
important influences on the trend toward sophistication at the local level,
including the sophistication of past campaigns for office, prior contact with
political consultants, and the level of competition. It appears that the electoral insecurity produced by a competitive race triggers the initial adoption
of sophisticated tactics in a particular local electoral district. In addition, candidates who have interacted with campaign professionals are more likely to
take this first innovative step. After new-style campaigns have been intro-
duced, both voters and reporters expect to see them in future races. As a
result, candidates have a strong tendency to imitate the strategies used by
their predecessors.

Perhaps the most notable finding of this chapter, however, is not overtly
contained in this final account of influences on local candidates' decisions. It
should be noted that all of the influences on candidates were found to promote the use of sophisticated tactics. Efforts to find factors suppressing the
adoption of new-style campaigns were futile. Candidates turned to new-style
activities just as often in states with a history of amateur politics. Traditional
support from political parties was also unrelated to candidates' contentment
with grassroots tactics. The lure of communication technology appears to be
persuasive, regardless of these circumstances.

In addition, the three strongest influences on candidates' decisions indicate that the trend toward sophisticated campaigns is both progressive and
irreversible. Competitive races are a sign of a healthy democracy. Few, if any,
reformers would advocate suppressing competition in order to prevent
encroaching sophistication. Yet as long as candidates face uncertain electoral
futures, some will attempt to improve their chances by turning to "new" tactics. Many of these innovative candidates will rely on the expertise of campaign professionals. The participation of consultants in local campaigns
simulates the activities of change agents. As potential adopters in these locali-

ties are exposed to consultants, they in turn become more innovative in their own electoral efforts. Finally, once the innovation has taken root, sophisticated tactics become expected activities in local campaigns. At this point, few candidates will voluntarily revert to traditional activities because they want to be perceived as serious contenders. According to this scenario, the trend toward new-style campaigns will gradually extend into more localities, and sophisticated tactics will eventually become permanent fixtures in many local electoral arenas. This prospect makes our understanding of how this particular trend will affect democracy in American localities all the more important. Consequently, chapter 4 examines more closely whether side effects have accompanied sophisticated campaigns into local political arenas.

Notes

1. Amy Argetsinger, "Crowded Field Running for Annapolis Mayor," *The Washington Post*, 14 September 1997, 5(B); and Brian Sullam, "Hopefuls in Annapolis Just Trying to Be Loved," *The Baltimore Sun*, 14 September 1997, 4(B).

2. Argetsinger, "Crowded Field Running for Annapolis Mayor," 5(B).

3. Argetsinger, "Crowded Field Running for Annapolis Mayor," 5(B); and Carl Snowden, Annapolis mayoral candidate, telephone interview by J. Cherie Strachan. Tape recording, September 2001.

4. Argetsinger, "Crowded Field Running for Annapolis Mayor," 5(B); Dan Thanh Dang, "Elections Board Investigating Possible Callahan Violations," *The Baltimore Sun*, 7 August 1997, 4(B); and Dennis Callahan telephone interview by J. Cherie Strachan. Tape recording, September 2001.

5. Callahan interview.

6. Argetsinger, "Crowded Field Running for Annapolis Mayor," 5(B).

7. As quoted by Dan Thanh Dang, "Perennial Candidate in Mayor's Race," *The Baltimore Sun*, 29 June 1997, 1(B).

8. Thanh Dang, "Perennial Candidate in Mayor's Race," 1(B).

9. As quoted by Thanh Dang, "Perennial Candidate in Mayor's Race," 1(B).

10. Dan Thanh Dang, "Ex-Mayor Callahan Edges Out Snowden," *The Baltimore Sun*, 17 September 1997, 1(A).

11. Dennis Johnson, Annapolis mayoral candidate, telephone interview by J. Cherie Strachan. Tape recording, September 2001.

12. Dan Thanh Dang, "Johnson Wins Mayor's Contest," *The Baltimore Sun*, 5 November 1997, 1(A).

13. Doris Graber, *Processing the News: How People Tame the Information Tide*, 2nd ed. (New York: Longman, 1988), 28.

14. Graber, *Processing the News*, 28.

15. Graber, *Processing the News*, 29.

16. Other researchers have summarized the number of professional services used to measure a similar concept, campaign professionalism. Herrnson relies on

House candidates' self-reports via a survey, while Medvic uses *Campaigns and Election* magazine's repeating feature, "Consultants' Scorecard," which reports the clientele of more prominent political consultants. This research counts sophisticated tactics instead, for a number of reasons. First, no comprehensive account of less prominent consultants and their local clientele is readily available, and resources were not available for an additional survey of the mayoral candidates. Second, although the political reporters interviewed provided an indicator of the types of consultants each mayoral candidate hired, they were far more confident—and less likely to claim "I don't know"—when describing the types of tactics used. See Paul Herrnson, "Hired Guns and House Races: Campaign Professionals in House Races," in *Campaign Warriors: The Role of Political Consultants in Elections,* ed. James A. Thurber and Candice J. Nelson (Washington: D.C.: Brookings Institution Press, 2000), 65–90; and Stephen K. Medvic, "Professionalization in Congressional Campaigns," in *Campaign Warriors: The Role of Political Consultants in Elections,* ed. James A. Thurber and Candice J. Nelson (Washington: D.C.: Brookings Institution Press, 2000), 91–109.

17. Other factors included on the list, but selected by only one or two consultants, include expectations of the electorate, use of tactics by an opponent, the new availability of a tactic, the desire to imitate other candidates, and the need to increase low voter-turnout rates.

18. Everett M. Rogers, *Diffusion of Innovations,* 3rd ed. (New York: Free Press, 1983), 166–67.

19. Rogers, *Diffusion of Innovations,* 166.

20. Rogers, *Diffusion of Innovations,* 258.

21. Rogers, *Diffusion of Innovations,* 313–16.

22. Daniel M. Shea, *Campaign Craft: The Strategies, Tactics and Art of Political Campaign Management* (Westport, Conn.: Praeger, 1996), 13.

23. Rogers, *Diffusion of Innovations,* 23.

24. These data were obtained from the U.S. Bureau of the Census, *County and City Databook: 1994* (Washington, D.C.: U.S. Government Printing Office, 1994).

25. Graber, *Processing the News,* 28.

26. Rogers, *Diffusion of Innovations,* 234–35.

27. Herrnson's description of how House candidates' perceptions of media coverage vary according to campaign professionalism supports this conclusion. Paul Herrnson, "Hired Guns and House Race: Campaign Professionals in House Elections," 85. Also see Anita Dunn, "The Best Campaign Wins: Local Press Coverage of Nonpresidential Races," in *Campaigns and Elections American Style,* ed. James A. Thurber and Candice J. Nelson (Boulder, Colo.: Westview, 1995), 113.

28. Dunn, "The Best Campaign Wins," 123.

29. Jay Jochnowitz, "Campaign Costs Up Stakes for Candidates," *Times Union* (Albany, N.Y.), 15 March 1998, 1(D) and 7(D).

30. Jochnowitz, "Campaign Costs Up Stakes for Candidates," 7(D).

31. Rogers, *Diffusion of Innovations,* 166.

32. Rogers, *Diffusion of Innovations,* 166.

33. Robert V. Friedenberg, *Communication Consultants in Political Campaigns* (Westport, Conn.: Praeger, 1997), 5.

34. Paul Grondahl, *Mayor Corning: Albany Icon, Albany Enigma* (Albany, N.Y.: Washington Park Press, 1997), 329.

35. Grondahl, *Mayor Corning,* 324; and Carl Touhey, Albany mayoral candidate, interview by J. Cherie Strachan. Tape recording, Albany, N.Y., May 1998.

36. Vic Ostrowidzki, "Corning Stays Unflappable in Reelection Bid," *Times Union* (Albany, N.Y.), 7 October 1973, 2(B).

37. Ostrowidzki, "Corning Stays Unflappable," 2(B).

38. Joe Picchi, "Quayle Poll Shows Touhey Leading," *Times Union* (Albany, N.Y.), 16 October 1973, 3; and Carol DeMare, "Touhey Claim on Taxes 'Reckless,' Corning Says," *Times Union* (Albany, N.Y.), 19 October 1973, 3.

39. Joe Picchi, "Mayor Walks, Touhey Talks." *Times Union* (Albany, N.Y.), 28 October 1973, 1(B).

40. Vic Ostrowidzki, "Mayoral Candidates Assess Chances," *Times Union* (Albany, N.Y.), 28 October 1973, 2(B).

41. "1973 Election Results," *Times Union* (Albany, N.Y.), 7 November 1973, 8; Also see Grondahl, *Mayor Corning,* 327, for claims of vote stealing.

42. Grondahl, *Mayor Corning,* 286.

43. Michael Muskal, "Nolan–Corning Fight Decision in 10 More Days," *Times Union* (Albany, N.Y.), 29 August 1977, 2; and Grondahl, *Mayor Corning,* 287.

44. Michael Muskal, "Albany Demo Primary Costs Top Record," *Times Union* (Albany, N.Y.), 1 October 1977, 3.

45. Daniel J. Elazar, *American Federalism: A View from the States* (New York: Thomas Y. Crowell, 1972), 90.

46. Elazar, *American Federalism,* 96–98.

47. Elazar, *American Federalism,* 98.

48. Tom Ragatz, Madison School Board candidate, telephone interview by J. Cherie Strachan. Tape recording, September 2001.

49. Ragatz interview; and "Sadly, Big Money Politics Comes to Town," *Capitol Times* (Madison, Wis.), 13 March 1997, 1(C).

50. Paul Norton, "Liberals Win School Race," *Capitol Times* (Madison, Wis.), 2 April 1997, 2(A).

51. Deborah Lawson, Madison School Board candidate, telephone interview by J. Cherie Strachan. Tape recording, October 2001.

52. "Sadly, Big Money Politics Comes to Town," 1(C).

53. Lawson interview.

54. Joseph Schlesinger, "The New American Political Party," *American Political Science Review* 79, no. 4 (December 1985): 1152–69.

55. Don Landers, Visalia mayor, telephone interview by J. Cherie Strachan. Tape recording, October 2001; and Lewis Griswold, "Visalia Council Race Shaping Up," *The Fresno Bee,* 4 July 1997, 1.

56. Cornelius P. Cotter, James L. Gibson, John F. Bibby, and Robert J. Huckshorn, *Party Organization in American Politics* (New York: Praeger, 1984).

57. See Paul Herrnson, "National Party Organizations at the Century's End," in *The Parties Respond,* ed. Sandy L. Maisel (Boulder, Colo.: Westview, 1998), 50–82; and John F. Bibby, "State Party Organizations: Coping and Adapting to Candidate Centered Politics and Nationalization," in *The Parties Respond,* ed. Sandy L. Maisel (Boulder, Colo: Westview, 1998), 23–49.

58. Brian F. Schaffner, Matthew J. Streb, and Gerald C. Wright, "A Rule That Works: The Nonpartisan Ballot in State and Local Elections" (paper presented at the annual meeting of the Midwest Political Science Association Meeting, Chicago, April 1999); and James B. Jamieson, "Some Social and Political Correlates of Incumbency in Municipal Elections," *Social Science Quarterly* 51, no. 4 (March 1971): 946–52.

59. Thomas Dye, *Politics in States and Communities,* 7th ed. (Englewood Cliffs, N.J.: Prentice Hall, 1991), 280.

How Will Encroaching Campaign Sophistication Affect the Health of Democracy?

4

Campaign Budgets Skyrocket in Howard County, Maryland

When first-term county councilman Dennis R. Schrader decided to run for an open county executive seat in 1998, he knew he faced an uphill battle. Unlike many politicians in Howard County, Maryland, population 247,842, Schrader was a relative newcomer to the area and lacked strong name recognition. To gauge how voters would react to his bid for county executive, he relied on focus groups and public opinion polls conducted by a nationally recognized polling firm. Although the results indicated a close race in the Republican primary, Schrader and his pollster believed that he could "close the gap." To do so, Schrader spent about $150,000 and launched a full array of new-style campaign tactics, including cable television spots, targeted direct mail, and a professionally maintained Internet site. These sophisticated tactics were combined with more traditional approaches, with the intention of driving up his name recognition. In fact, Schrader believes that he gained the edge needed to win the primary election by canvassing door-to-door. Yet he spent an additional $80,000 during the general election and even turned to broadcast television in the Baltimore market in his efforts to increase support.[1]

Although the Democratic candidate, former police chief James N. Robey, ran unopposed in the primary, he began airing three cable television commercials to remind voters that there would be a Democratic choice in the general election.[2] Robey spent $82,000, some of which was paid to a pollster. The remainder of the new-style tactics used on his campaign, however, were enacted without professional expertise. His television advertisements and direct mail pieces were all designed internally, with firms hired only to provide production, printing, and distribution services. Since he did not have time to canvass extensively, Robey also relied heavily on newspaper advertisements, including full-page ads as the general election neared.[3]

Robey, who was endorsed by Schrader's Republican primary opponent, went on to win the general election. Despite his campaign's success without professional consultants, attitudes toward campaigning in Howard County have been altered. Robey's campaign adviser predicted that future candidates—including any candidates she advises—will turn to communication technology and expertise as long as they can afford it.[4] Meanwhile, another local politician, who was critical of funds both candidates' collected from developers, was quoted in the local paper as claiming that an effective candidate for county executive must now raise at least $100,000. "You can be the nicest, sweetest guy, but you are not going to win. . . . Big checks are very important," he said.[5]

Unintended Consequences of Campaign Sophistication

This account demonstrates the way that sophisticated campaigns have made inroads into America's local political arenas. In addition, data presented in the previous chapter indicate that their presence in smaller electoral districts will most certainly expand with each election cycle. The candidates who decide to adopt new-style strategies are thinking primarily of their own electoral security. In competitive races, candidates turn to new tactics to gain an edge over their competitors because they want to win. Similarly, candidates use sophisticated tactics and hire political consultants in order to achieve the status of serious contenders. Yet their decisions have ramifications beyond their own immediate success or failure. New-style campaigns fundamentally change the way elections are won. Running for office becomes more complex, and once-sufficient resources are no longer adequate. A successful campaign relies on an array of resources to persuade voters. Examples include a charismatic candidate, the candidate's time, volunteer support, and, of course, an ample budget. In the past, candidates lacking access to one resource could more easily compensate with another. When new-style campaigns took root in national and statewide races, however, the importance of money was enhanced at the expense of other resources.

A similar effect in local elections could restrict citizens' access to the process in the venue traditionally most amenable to their participation. Not only would fewer people be capable of becoming competitive candidates for public offices, but average citizens might find it more difficult to make meaningful contributions to candidates' efforts. Candidates' reliance on new channels of communication also has the potential to revolutionize interactions between candidates and citizens, including the latter's ability to hold elected officers accountable. New-style campaigns may affect this ability by altering the type of contact that occurs between candidates and voters, the amount of information disseminated by candidates, and the content of politicians' messages.

Hence, candidates' decisions have broad consequences for the health of electoral processes. And, as the examples further on reveal, they are not related to a passing fad, but to altered definitions of what constitutes the "bare necessities" of a local campaign. When the candidates who choose to go sophisticated win, these new definitions are only reinforced.

New-Style Campaigning a "Necessity" in Albany, New York, and Tacoma, Washington

Detrimental effects of new-style campaigns stem from the development of a perceived need for sophisticated tactics. Technically, advanced communication technology is not required for local candidates to interact with their constituencies. Grassroots activities are not only feasible, but are more persuasive. Yet for the reasons outlined in chapter 3, sophisticated tactics can come to be perceived as essential to winning local government races. A comparison of comments about the two most recent mayoral races in Albany, New York, demonstrates just how quickly such needs can be developed. In 1993, the incumbent mayor stepped down, resulting in an open race for the all-important Democratic Party nomination. Of the candidates who threw their hats into the ring, Harold Joyce was viewed by many as the party favorite. As the chair of the City Democratic Committee, he was seen as the obvious heir to the throne. (Despite predictions of his success, he lost the primary election.) With this quasi-incumbent status, political pundits speculated that Joyce easily had the capacity to raise $250,000 for the race. A local public relations specialist who had worked on numerous campaigns in the Albany area, however, warned that Joyce would risk appearing imprudent if he spent such a large amount. He claimed: "I think it's going to be hard and . . . almost irresponsible to spend that kind of money in the city of Albany."[6] Four years later, however, the losing mayoral candidate was chastised by local politicians, reporters, and campaign professionals for failing to do just that.

The loser of Albany's 1997 Democratic primary for mayor was incumbent New York assemblyman John ("Jack") McEneny. While the mayor spent over $400,000 on a sophisticated campaign, relying heavily on outside professional assistance, McEneny ran a low-budget, simple campaign utilizing grassroots activities such as canvassing, yard signs, and literature drops. His campaign staff consisted primarily of his immediate family members. His campaign manager, for example, was his college-aged daughter. The campaign aired three different radio advertisements, yet all were developed internally without professional assistance. His campaign committee also managed to broadcast, at the tail end of the campaign, a single television commercial filmed by the candidate's son that suffered in comparison to the mayor's blitz of expertly crafted television advertising. Assistance from professionals was precluded by McEneny's self-imposed campaign contribution limit. Much to his daughter's dismay, he refused to accept more than $500 from any single contributor until the last few weeks of the campaign.[7] After the election, he claimed, "I wanted this to be a hometown race that can be waged in the neighborhoods and on the front porches. The major scandal in America is the selling of city halls, county courthouses and even legislative seats."[8]

As a result of these decisions, the effectiveness of McEneny's campaign was questioned throughout the race. A reporter for a local alternative newspaper noted, "No one really wants to take McEneny to task publicly on this point, but it's believed that his home-style, old-fashioned approach was simply inadequate against a moneyed incumbent with a team of hired guns at his disposal."[9] Meanwhile, a local political consultant argued, "Jack didn't want to do the kinds of things candidates have to do. It's commendable to run a race on $50,000, but when the opponent has $400,000 he sets the rules, and that's what happened in this race."[10] Within the space of four years, a single election cycle, raising $250,000 had gone from an imprudent undertaking apt to generate resentment from the electorate to a strategic necessity. Four years earlier, before Jennings's campaign set a new standard, McEneny's approach may have been taken more seriously. Yet in 1997 his efforts paled in comparison to those of the incumbent. McEneny aptly described the effect of the city's altered expectations when he said, "The problem is that perception is reality, and if the perception is one of a lackluster campaign, then it becomes reality."[11] After observing McEneny's loss and the reaction to his campaign, future mayoral candidates in Albany will surely assume that a new-style campaign strategy is indeed an essential element of a winning mayoral campaign in Albany.

Apparently, this shift in expectations has also taken place in Tacoma, Washington, population 193,556. When term limits resulted in a vacant mayoral seat in 2001, six candidates threw their hats into the ring. The three candidates who failed to hire professional consultants were easily defeated. One failed to submit adequate signatures and was disqualified prior to the nonpartisan primary election.[12] The remaining two unsophisticated candidates, who had minimal campaign budgets of only $797 and $587 each, shared 16 percent of the primary vote.[13] Meanwhile, the top three vote-getters in the primary spent between $39,013 and $67,681 apiece, and they all hired either local or Seattle-based political consultants.[14]

Local Campaigning Becomes an ''Arms Race''

When new-style candidates like those in Tacoma, Washington, win, the perceived need for sophisticated tactics is reinforced and becomes a self-fulfilling prophecy. Information gathered about mayoral candidates in midsized cities indicates that such outcomes are not unique. Mayoral candidates with more sophisticated campaigns often defeated their opponents. To determine the effect of varying levels of sophistication between opposing mayoral candidates, the differences between competing candidates' campaign sophistication were compared. Some candidates used as many as three fewer sophisticated tactics than did their opponents. Yet the majority (56 percent) of candidates relied on identical numbers of sophisticated tactics. Twenty-four percent, however, relied on fewer tactics than their opponents, whereas 20 percent used more. (These two percentages are not identical because ten mayoral races had more than two mayoral candidates.) When candidates relied on the same number of sophisticated tactics, they had similar success rates. Fifty-seven percent of the winning candidates relied on the same number of sophisticated tactics as their opponents did, but so did 54 percent of losing candidates. On the other hand, a clear pattern emerged when candidates had access to more sophisticated tactics. Of the winning candidates, 32 percent had more sophisticated campaigns. Meanwhile, only 10 percent of losing candidates relied on more sophisticated tactics than did their successful competitors. Keep in mind that even a modest pattern between sophistication and success will have a strong impact on candidates. Office seekers who are "out-gunned" by sophisticated opponents are more apt to lose on election day. Hence, prospective candidates assume that they must at least match the efforts of their opponents in order to improve their chances of winning. The "arms race" mentality generated by these assumptions guarantees that this trend will not be short-lived, which means that the accompanying consequences need to be assessed.

Consequences for Citizen Access to the Electoral Process

The complexity of new-style campaigns, as well as their emphasis on spending, raises the threshold of information and financial resources that potential candidates need in order to enter the electoral arena. Not all potential candidates, especially those who lack either experience or wealth, will feel up to the task. This phenomenon has been described as the innovativeness–needs paradox. In short, "those individuals . . . in a social system who most need the benefits of a new technological idea (the less educated, less wealthy, and the like) are generally the last to adopt that innovation. The units in a system who adopt first generally least need the benefits of the innovation."[15] Unfortunately, new-style local campaigns will benefit the types of candidates who already have an edge over their opponents.

The Advantages of Incumbency and Socioeconomic Status

Since incumbents have at least one successful campaign effort under their belts, one should expect them to incorporate the communication technologies associated with winning. The data collected on mayoral candidates in midsized cities indicate that challenged incumbents do incorporate sophisticated tactics more frequently than do their opponents. This pattern is demonstrated most clearly by looking at contested races because it focuses attention on activities undertaken in serious re-election efforts. Even when incumbents have the capacity to go sophisticated, those with secure seats probably will not be inclined to make the effort.

To identify the types of candidates in each race, newspapers' political reporters were asked whether competition in their cities involved candidates running for an open seat or incumbents facing challengers. Thirty-three percent of the candidates were opposed incumbents, and 36 percent were challengers. Twenty-seven percent were running in open seats, while 4 percent were unchallenged incumbents.

The candidates who turned to sophisticated tactics most frequently were those running in open seats, as 81 percent of them relied on at least two or more sophisticated tactics. This pattern results from the intense competition typically characterizing open seat races. Ambitious candidates are often more willing to throw their hats into the ring when they do not have to face an incumbent. Opposed incumbents, however, were the second-most sophisticated type of candidates, as 71 percent relied on two or more tactics. In comparison, their opponents were much less successful at incorporating the trappings of new-style campaigns into their efforts. Twenty percent fewer of the challengers facing these incumbent mayors races relied on two or more sophisticated tactics. Finally, unopposed incumbents, who have little need to campaign seriously as their re-election is guaranteed, were the least sophisticated candidates. Only 30 percent relied on two or more sophisticated tactics.[16] Obviously, the most concerning difference in the use of sophisticated tactics is the gap between incumbents and challengers.

Similar to incumbents, candidates with higher social class status typically have broader past experiences and access to better financial resources with the potential to provide electoral advantages. To explore the possibility of such an effect, the social class of each mayoral candidate was measured by asking reporters to indicate whether they belonged to the lower, middle, or upper class. Many reporters insisted on describing candidates as "upper-middle class," and consequently this category was incorporated into list of possible responses. Only 3 percent of mayoral candidates were described as belonging to the lower class. This finding is understandable, as a certain threshold of resources has always been needed to engage in political activity. The bulk of mayoral candidates (68 percent) was described as middle class. However, reporters indicated that 13 percent had upper-middle-class status, while 16 percent were classified as upper class.[17] Those candidates perceived by reporters as belonging to the upper-middle and upper classes were more apt to adopt new-style activities. Eighty-five percent of them relied on two or more sophisticated tactics, while only 64 percent of those classified as middle or lower class did likewise.

EXACERBATING THE GAP IN REPRESENTATION   In the United States, election to a local office is often a stepping-stone to state or national positions. For example, researchers have predicted the future number of female members of Congress based on how many women hold state elective offices.[18] Hence, excluding an entire class of candidates from local government races could further widen the socioeconomic gap between the electorate and their public officials and could affect the representativeness of all U.S. governing institutions. From this perspective, such patterns are disconcerting. Incumbents and upper-class candidates have always had an edge in amassing the resources needed to run for office. Yet the trend toward new-style campaigns further enhances their inherent advantages. As sophistication becomes associated with success, those candidates most capable of incorporating communication technology will benefit. Potential candidates lacking the advantages of incumbency and higher social class status may be intimidated by the prospect of a new-style campaign and may decide not to run for office. For those who do enter political races, persuading others to take their efforts seriously will be more difficult for them.

The Source of Advantages—Fundraising

Much of the advantage enjoyed by incumbents and wealthier candidates surely stems from the increased budgets associated with new-style campaigns. The falling cost of technology, as well as competition among increasing numbers of political consultants, brought the cost of new-style campaigns into more local candidates' price ranges. Yet incorporating sophisticated tactics and hiring professionals still drive up the overall cost of local campaigns. Advertising time is much less expensive on cable television than on the major networks. Nevertheless, producing television advertisements and purchasing inexpensive cable airtime still cost more than canvassing door-to-door. While money is a welcome resource, regardless of campaign style, it is less essential in old-style campaigns. Money may help to stock campaign headquarters and to print campaign literature, yet grassroots activities can be carried out without access to large amounts of money. New-style campaigns, on the other hand, run on the generalized resource of money, which is needed to purchase technology and expertise.

The fundraising advantage enjoyed by incumbents has been well documented.[19] Incumbents can contact people who donated to previous campaigns, and they may even have war chests of unspent funds from previous races. In addition, people and organizations who donate money in order to maintain access to officeholders, rather than for ideological reasons, overwhelmingly give to incumbents. "Because incumbents are usually expected to prevail, they receive the lion's share of contributions."[20] Those with high socioeconomic status are also better prepared to approach the task of raising money. When candidates fundraise, the first piece of advice they usually receive is to build a file of potential donors, beginning with their family members, friends, and professional associates.[21] Candidates with higher socioeconomic status and a network of professional associates will obviously be able to generate a much larger list. Moreover, their associates tend to share their socioeconomic status, thereby making them capable of donating larger amounts of money. Incumbency and upper-class advantages emerge, in part, because these candidates find it easier to raise the money needed to purchase communication technology and expertise.

The expenditure patterns of mayoral candidates in midsized cities indicate that sophistication is in fact related to higher campaign spending at the local level. To determine the size of mayoral candidates' budgets, reporters were asked to approximate how much money candidates spent on their electoral efforts. Some looked up the precise amounts in old newspaper stories, while others felt comfortable estimating them.[22] Candidate spending ranged from the three candidates who spent nothing at all to the incumbent mayor of Jersey City, New Jersey, who spent approximately $1 million. Yet referring to this figure as representative of all the mayoral candidates' spending would be misleading because it is unusually high. For example, the next-highest amount spent was $550,000. Only 4 percent of the mayoral candidates spent more than $300,000, and only 15 percent spent more than $150,000. The bulk of the candidates, 79 percent, spent $100,000 or less. Meanwhile, many mayoral candidates had comparatively small campaign budgets. Twenty-five percent spent less than $15,000, and 52 percent spent less than $40,000.

Table 4.1 lists the average amount spent by candidates with varying levels of campaign sophistication. It reveals, as has occurred elsewhere in the U.S. political system, that spending increases as more new-style activities are adopted. Candidates who relied on all four sophisticated tactics spent an average amount of $111,773 more than those who relied on none. Each additional tactic adopted is related to an increase in average spending of at least $10,471 and as much as $65,820. This finding should come as no surprise. It mimics the impact of new-style campaigning on campaign budgets in state and national election campaigns. Increased spending occurs because new-style campaigns require money, which is needed to purchase communication technology, as well as the assistance of experts who know how to use it most effectively.

The Financial Benefits of Incumbency

Examples drawn from Albany's political history document the fundraising advantages of incumbency. Albany's Jerry Jennings, for instance, experienced the financial benefits of incumbency immediately after winning the 1993 Democratic primary election. At the urging of a state senator who supported Jennings, the state comptroller sponsored a $500-per-head fundraiser for him at a Manhattan nightclub. The event was intended to help Jennings pay off his $23,000 debt from the primary and to introduce him to "some influential people in finance and development."[23] The state senator supporting Jennings said, "Even though Jerry won the primary, he still has bills to pay."[24] Prior to the event, Jennings had not seen the invitations and knew virtually none of the guests who attended. As a dark horse candidate, he was unable to attract such financial support on his own. Yet after winning the Democratic mayoral primary in New York's capitol city, which guaranteed his eventual win in the general election, Jennings garnered the backing of influential politicians and the contributions of their financial supporters.

Data collected about mayoral candidates in midsized cities indicate that incumbents in cities across the country experience similar fundraising successes. Table 4.2 lists the average amount of money spent by various types of candidates. It clearly illustrates that challenged incumbents far outspend other types of candidates. Not surprisingly, unopposed incumbents with little to fear had minimal campaign budgets. Note that while open seat candidates incorporated more sophisticated tactics than did other types of candidates, they still did not approach the spending power of opposed incumbents. Challenged incumbents' average spending was $34,855 more than open seat candidates. The most troubling difference presented in the table, however, is the gap between spending by incumbents and their challengers. The average amount spent by challengers is only 61 percent of the average amount spent

Table 4.1   Increased Spending Linked to Sophistication

# of Sophisticated Tactics	Average Spending
0	$ 17,158
1	$ 27,629
2	$ 48,315
3	$114,135
4	$128,931

Notes: To prevent skewing, the candidate who spent $1 million was excluded. The sophisticated tactics counted in this table were public opinion polls, television ads, targeted direct mail, and radio ads.
Source: 1998 interviews about the most recent mayoral candidates in midsized cities.

by their incumbent opponents. Challengers have a difficult burden to over-come. Their spending deficit makes it harder for them to purchase tactics typ-ically used in new-style campaigns and to be perceived as serious candidates.

The Financial Benefits of Socioeconomic Status

Those with higher social class status enjoy a fundraising advantage similar to that of incumbents. When contributors are scarce, for example, wealthy can-didates are capable of funding their own efforts. This scenario is precisely what happened in Albany's 1973 mayoral race.

Carl Touhey, the local businessman who decided to oppose the machine-supported incumbent, accepted the Republican Party's nomination. At this point in the city's history, however, political resources were dominated by the Democratic Party machine. According to Touhey, people were afraid to volunteer their time or to donate their money to maverick candidates for fear of retribution. Local businesses even feared that failing to follow the machine's rules of the game would result in economic consequences.[25] For example, Touhey claimed that he was motivated to run for mayor after being cut out of legitimate business deals. Touhey owned the oldest and largest Ford dealership in the region, but the city never bought vehicles from him.[26] He described the municipal bidding process with the following account: "The thing was rigged and we knew Dan [the chair of the Democratic County Party Committee] was getting some kind of kickback, but we didn't lower ourselves. We refused to bow and scrape before the machine to get their handout, because that meant you owed them your vote and more."[27]

Touhey was a wealthy entrepreneur who owned several other businesses, including a soft drink bottling plant. During debates, he revealed that his yearly salary was approximately $100,000 and his net worth was over $1 mil-lion.[28] In short, he was far from the typical Albany resident. Ordinary citizens who may have been disgusted with the Albany machine had limited abilities to mount a serious opposition. They would have had difficulty amassing enough volunteers or contributions to be effective. Touhey, however, had

Table 4.2   The Financial Advantage of Incumbency

Candidate Status	Average Spending
Unopposed Incumbent	$ 14,527
Challenger	$ 61,294
Open Seat	$ 66,418
Opposed Incumbent	$101,273

Note: To prevent skewing, this average excludes the candidate who spent $1,000,000.
Source: 1998 interviews about the most recent mayoral candidates in midsized cities.

the financial capacity to devise an alternative strategy. He turned to communication technology and professional assistance to communicate his message to the voters, and he paid for the effort out of his own pocket. Touhey estimates that he spend between $50,000 and $70,000 on the campaign, of which 95 percent was his own money.[29]

In 1973, he ran a new-style campaign that would make many current candidates envious. According to newspaper accounts, for example, Touhey was the first local candidate in Albany's history to hire a professional pollster.[30] Information garnered from the polls was used by the advertising specialists to produce a full array of newspaper and television advertisements.[31] Touhey probably felt comfortable relying on the electronic media because he had used them to promote his commercial enterprises. Hence, financial independence enabled Touhey not only to mount a serious campaign against the invincible Albany machine and Mayor Corning, but to come within a hairbreadth of winning the race.

Many reformers criticize current campaign finance practices because they enable wealthy candidates to continue expressing political opinions regardless of their ability to attract supporters. While this concern is legitimate, Touhey's participation had a positive effect on Albany politics. The machine's stranglehold on the electoral process prevented competitive races and denied Albany residents the ability to hold elected officers accountable. In this environment, he expressed opinions that others shared, but were afraid to admit. His near-success was the first chink in the machine's armor and encouraged later candidates to continue opposing the status quo. Despite this contribution, the point of telling the story of his campaign is to emphasize that he was an effective candidate only because he could afford to spend nearly $70,000 of his own money. Equally disgruntled citizens of more modest means could not undertake a serious campaign for mayor. Although Touhey's campaign was beneficial, any political environment creating such a substantial burden on potential candidates cannot be described as a healthy democracy.

Touhey's sophisticated efforts, when traditional campaign resources were dominated by the machine, provide an extreme example of the benefits of social class status. The amount of money needed to wage mayoral campaigns in Albany has, however, been a more recent issue in the city. In 1993, a potential mayoral candidate explicitly cited financial concerns in his decision not to run in the Democratic mayoral primary election. Unlike the 1973 race, these financial concerns were imposed by encroaching sophistication. Albany alderman Keith St. John had achieved widespread name recognition throughout the city and the nation as the first openly homosexual black elected official. He briefly considered parlaying this name recognition into a bid for mayor. When informing reporters of his decision to remain an alderman, St. John "acknowledged that with expectations that the mayor's race could run

$300,000 or more per candidate, the finances were out of his reach."[32] For candidates with financial independence or a circle of wealthy associates, such fundraising hurdles are less burdensome.

Data gathered on mayoral candidates in midsized cities support the conclusion that upper-class candidates face fewer financial limitations. The average amount spent by candidates perceived as upper-middle and upper class by reporters was $75,812 more than spent by their counterparts with lower-class backgrounds. The former spent an average of $129,984, while the latter spent, on average, only $54,172. In other words, the average amount spent by lower- and middle-class candidates was only 42 percent of higher-class candidates' average campaign budget.

FINANCIAL RESOURCES LINKED TO SUCCESS   Finally, their access to sophisticated tactics and financial support appears to have a positive impact on incumbents' and upper-class candidates' success rates. In the 72 races where incumbent mayors faced challengers, only 15 percent of the incumbents lost. The number of races where reporters perceived a difference in opposing candidates' social class status was smaller. In all but 20 races, candidates had identical class status. Yet in these 20 races, candidates with higher class status had a clear advantage and lost only 25 percent of the races. In addition, all but one of the five losing upper-class candidates were challengers, and no higher class candidates lost when they outranked their opponents by two or three class categories.

These findings suggest that the trend toward new-style campaigns is raising the threshold of financial and information resources necessary to run successfully for local government offices. As a result, the advantages previously enjoyed by particular types of candidates are exacerbated. The occurrence of such patterns in midsized cities is especially troubling. The success of candidates with lower- and middle-class backgrounds enhances the representativeness of democratic institutions. Yet if these candidates are not "learning the ropes" by holding local offices, either because they are intimidated out of the electoral process or because they are apt to lose, fewer will attempt bids for state and national positions.

An Intimidating War Chest in Cherokee County, Georgia

The following account of an underfunded challenger in Cherokee County, Georgia, population 141,903, reveals how intimidating an incumbent's fundraising capacity can be. In 1998, Emily Lemke became concerned that her home county was taking on too much development. When the County Commission failed to address her concerns, she decided to run for office. Since the commissioner in her own district was not up for re-election, Lemke decided to challenge incumbent county chairman Hollis Lathem.[33] (She was joined by another slow-growth challenger, bringing the total number of candidates in the nonpartisan primary election to three.) Lathem, whose family has been involved in Cherokee County politics for generations, was capable of raising an intimidating war chest. For the primary election alone, Lathem raised $105,387 and spent $64,108. Ample funds enabled him to pay a political consultant $20,000, hire a polling firm, advertise on television, and send out several mailings.[34] His spending prompted a local political reporter to write, "Lathem's two foes can only hope that his huge cash advantage doesn't translate into votes."[35]

Lemke, who spent only $5,455 during the primary, did not expect to defeat Lathem, but believed that she had a moral obligation to run. "I thought someone needed to present an option," she said. Perhaps to both her and her opponents' surprise, no candidate won enough votes to claim victory in the primary election, resulting in a run-off between Lathem and Lemke. Lemke refused to fundraise, but did accept donations from those attending her speaking engagements. She spent an additional $17,500 on mailings and yard signs during the run-off, but never hired any professional assistance. In fact, she served as her own campaign manager. Her alternative to expensive advertising was to gather volunteers with signs at a busy intersection during rush hour traffic. The signs, similar to 1950s Burma Shave signs, relayed ever-changing catchy jingles. One example was: Does this traffic get your goat? Then let Lemke get your vote![36]

Lemke, an underfunded housewife, defeated Lathem and is now serving her first term as chair of Cherokee County. She remains undecided about whether to run for re-election, but insists that she will not run a sophisticated race even as an incumbent. "I won't take money from developers, so where would I get the money?" she questioned.[37] Lemke's unexpected success serves as a refreshing reminder that underdogs sometimes win. But it is important to note that she ran to make a point, not because she expected to defeat a well-funded incumbent. Other potential candidates may be less willing to face such odds.

SCARING AWAY POTENTIAL CANDIDATES   Tracking down those who have refused to run because of the trend toward new-style campaigns is a difficult task. Yet newspaper accounts provide some evidence that this negative side effect has occurred. One letter to the editor in the *Las Vegas Review Journal* read, "Recent stories about fund raising for county commission races reveal something absolutely reprehensible. If the average citizen wishes to run for a seat, it is next to impossible given the financial demands."[38] In another story on the 1993 campaigns for the Jefferson County, Colorado (population 527,056), Board of Education, one candidate's political consultant claimed that the average citizen "has been priced out of the ability to run in this race."[39] Another candidate, who complained that the high stakes might drive him out of the race, said, "I'm not going to take out a mortgage on my house."[40] This side effect of intimidating potential candidates out of politics is problematic because it appears to narrow a traditional point of access for the politically ambitious. Unfortunately, the pattern will in all likelihood be enhanced as the trend toward sophisticated local campaigns becomes more entrenched.

Consequences for Citizens' Abilities to Make Meaningful Campaign Contributions

A second concern related to the increased campaign spending typically associated with new-style campaigns is the potential to enhance the influence of wealthy contributors. The use of these campaigns in national and state politics has made it necessary for candidates "to solicit money on their own behalf—and to do so vigorously."[41] In order to raise additional money required for sophisticated efforts, candidates replace or supplement small, individual donations with larger contributions. Yet this fundraising strategy creates the impression, if not the reality, of candidates who are beholden to a few big contributors. This concern is exacerbated in smaller electoral districts. Numerous well-funded groups tend to vie for the attention of state and national government officials. According to James Madison in *Federalist Number 10*, the multiplicity of factions in larger political communities will counteract each single faction's influence. In smaller, more homogenous communities, however, the number of factions vying for political favors decreases.[42] The lack of competition increases the probability that specific special interests will gain influence, especially if candidates believe that they need special interests' financial support in order to run competitive races. Even if elected officials do not favor wealthy special interests, large contributions often make voters suspicious that money matters more than votes, which decreases their sense of political efficacy.

Shifting Fundraising Patterns in Albany, New York

Specific examples of such shifts in fundraising strategies can be drawn from Albany's 1993 and 1997 mayoral races. When Jerry Jennings won the Democratic primary in 1993, he realized that he needed to alter his fundraising strategy in order to pay his debts from the primary and to maintain a television presence throughout the general election. As a result, he allowed state politicians to organize the previously described Manhattan cocktail party, even though he had been an outspoken critic of such events. Throughout his tenure as an alderman, Jennings had roundly criticized similar fundraising activities. For example, once the prior incumbent mayor held a $500 per couple event; according to newspaper accounts, Jennings argued that the mayor was "catering to the limousine class again and excluding the little people of the Democratic Party."[43] He made similar claims about his 1993 primary opponent after Joyce held a $1,000-a-plate breakfast. Jennings said, "I just hope when they were cutting up their ham and eggs at breakfast, they weren't cutting up the city of Albany. . . . What is the intent of a $1,000 contribution?"[44]

Until he won the primary election, Jennings maintained the image of a "common man" with little tolerance for raising funds. One pundit described him with the following statement: "Jerry, who is comfortable going door-to-door talking to voters, is uncomfortable raising money or convincing the power structure he's the guy."[45] The Manhattan fundraiser signaled a turning point in his attitude toward campaign finance. He admitted to local reporters that the fundraiser made him feel uncomfortable, but naively said, "Maybe it was just to introduce me to some people that might be interested in doing some things for the City of Albany."[46] Notably present at the event were representatives from a development firm with projects in Albany, as well as the senior vice president of a company interested in building an incinerator at the Port of Albany.[47]

As his 1997 campaign budget indicates, Jennings was more comfortable raising money as an incumbent than he was as a dark horse challenger. The sources of his contributions in both mayoral races are summarized in table 4.3, which shows that he raised $274,397 more for his re-election bid than for his 1993 campaign. In order to raise this amount of money, Jennings altered his fundraising strategies by relying on new sources of income. This alteration, however, is not apparent in the percentage of funds raised from different sources. In 1993, Jennings raised 57 percent of his money from individuals, while in 1997 the amount constituted 62 percent of his budget. Similarly, the percentage of his budget from business organizations shifted only slightly, from 28 percent to 32 percent. Jennings still raised a substantial amount of money from small individual contributions in 1997, as an impressive $222,735 was amassed from individual contributions of $500 or less. Note while the cut-off of contributions included in this category was a substantial $500, a review of Jennings's campaign finance reports reveals that many were far smaller. He was known, for example, to hold "hot dog and beer" fundraisers, which many residents could afford to attend. Furthermore, the sum of money he raised in contributions of $1,000 or more (from all types of donors) was nearly identical in both races. In 1993 he raised $23,075 in such large amounts, while the 1997 figure was $26,550. One cannot claim that Jennings was not supported by individual citizens, or that his re-election efforts were solely dependent on contributions from special interests and wealthy individuals.

However, other patterns of change clearly emerge. The percentage of support provided by labor unions dropped substantially. Meanwhile, the sum of money that Jennings raised from business sources alone in 1997 approached his overall 1993 campaign budget. Finally, Jennings did increase his reliance on larger contributions in 1997, as the funds raised from contributions of more than $500 (from all types of donors) jumped substantially. In 1993 the amount raised from contributions of more than $500 was only $37,625, while in 1997 it was $106,550.

Admittedly, Jennings could still have waged a more moderate new-style campaign with small donations from individual citizens. He would not, however, have been able to raise his record-breaking 1997 war chest without the contributions from special interest groups and wealthy individuals. Their financial assistance pushed his campaign budget over the top. The research design employed in the examination of Albany mayoral races did not track whether such contributors received preferential treatment of any sort. But when his 1997 opponent, Jack McEneny, criticized Jennings for "selling city hall," Jennings told a reporter, "That's political nonsense. I don't know who has given money. I don't want to know. It's not necessary to know."[48]

Yet to some extent, whether Jennings knew of large donors' contributions or treated them differently may be irrelevant. If voters had been aware of his fundraising coups, they might have become suspicious. Ironically, the same technology responsible for increasing campaign budgets enables opponents to broadcast criticisms of each others' fundraising efforts. Average citizens cannot afford to make such sizable contributions. When candidates alter their campaign finance strategies to wage sophisticated campaigns, voters come to believe that the influence they achieve is overpowered. Hence, the campaign finance practices accompanying new-style campaigns diminish the electorate's sense of political efficacy.

Table 4.3   The Incumbency Advantage in Albany

Type of Donor	Contributions to Challenger Jennings (1993)		Contributions to Mayor Jennings (1977)	
	%	Amount	%	Amount
Individuals	57	$ 96,711	62	$274,435
Businesses	28	$ 48,278	32	$144,116
Labor	15	$ 24,675	4	$ 16,460
Other	—		2	$ 9,050
Total		$169,664		$444,061

Source: Campaign finance reports filed with the Albany County Board of Elections.

Yet candidates, who are focused on winning on election day, need money in order to compete effectively. McEneny's actions late in the 1997 campaign season provide another example of how the pressure to adopt new-style tactics affects fundraising strategies. As an incumbent member of the Assembly, McEneny could have attracted large contributions from the outset of his mayoral campaign. A strident critic of campaign finance practices, he tried to set an example by capping donations at $500 per contributor. Late in the campaign, however, McEneny acknowledged that his message was being overwhelmed by the incumbent's media blitz. He capitulated to his campaign manager's requests and began accepting larger contributions; the money helped pay for a last-minute television commercial.[49] In the closing weeks of the campaign, McEneny accepted $7,300 in large contributions from Democratic members of the Assembly. The amount represented 12 percent of his overall budget. Of this sum, $2,300 was donated by a member from the Bronx, while another assemblyman from Brooklyn gave $1,000.[50] Given the traditional conflict between upstate New York (where Albany is located) and New York City, such contributions are just as likely to raise voters' suspicions as are those from special interests. Few Albany residents would be pleased with a mayoral candidate whom they perceived to be beholden to New York City politicians. This account emphasizes the fact that even candidates with good intentions alter their fundraising strategies when they believe they need to adopt sophisticated tactics in order to compete effectively.

Shifting Fundraising Patterns in Midsized Cities

To determine whether local candidates outside the city of Albany made similar fundraising decisions, reporters were questioned about the primary sources of their mayoral candidates' funds. They were asked to select the most important source of candidates' financial support from the following list: individual contributions under $500, individual contributions over $500, organizations (including businesses), political parties, or personal money. In common with Jerry Jennings, most mayoral candidates appeared to have mixed fundraising strategies because reporters insisted that they relied on more than one source for their contributions.

It is reassuring to find that most mayors, 63 percent, were described as relying on small individual contributions of under $500. This category was by far the most frequently cited source of mayoral candidates' money. Again, the cap of $500 overestimates the size of individual contributions summarized in this category. Reporters often expanded on their selection by explaining that mayoral candidates' finance efforts were unpretentious fundraisers with minimal cover charges. Thus, many candidates appear to fund their campaigns by obtaining widespread support from members of their community. Far fewer candidates, 40 percent, were perceived as dependent on organizations for funds, although this percentage still represents a substantial number of mayoral candidates. Larger individual contributions or personal money were tied as even more infrequent sources of funds, as only 16 percent of candidates were described as reliant on either of these two types of contributions. Finally, signaling the candidate-centered nature of today's campaigns, as well as the popularity of nonpartisan local elections, only a small minority of mayoral candidates, 4 percent, were described as deriving a substantial portion of their funds from a political party.

Despite the preponderance of candidates turning to small individual contributions, fundraising strategies might still vary with campaign sophistication. To identify any such patterns, the relationships between reliance on particular types of donors and campaign sophistication were examined. A slight negative relationship was documented between the use of personal money and sophistication levels. Perhaps this pattern occurs because candidates who cannot attract supporters end up spending their own money, but as a result they cannot afford advanced communication technology. Meanwhile, both types of individual contributions have negligible relationships to sophistication. This pattern should be expected for small individual contributions. Yet, apparently, candidates with new-style campaigns are no more apt to rely on large individual contributions than are those making more traditional efforts. The relationship between political party contributions and sophistication was also very weak. The most notable relationship was between organizational contributions and sophistication. For example, of the mayoral candidates who relied on only one or fewer sophisticated tactics, organizations were primary donors for 34 percent. For those who incorporated two or more sophisticated tactics, this percentage increased to 42 percent. One final piece of evidence indicating that fundraising strategies evolve to meet the increased financial need created by new-style campaigns was obtained by comparing the most recent mayoral candidates in midsized cities to their predecessors. As previously indicated, political candidates have a strong tendency to imitate the activities of prior office seekers. Hence, these comparisons help to determine whether variations from predecessors' fundraising patterns are related to shifts from their campaign styles. By doing so, they place each recent candidate's behavior in the context of his or her city's political history.

Reporters were asked to identify the typical financial sources of their respective city's previous three mayoral candidates.[51] These responses were combined with previously requested information about prior candidates' tactics to identify any patterns between financial sources and sophistication. Not surprisingly, almost all recent candidates' fundraising patterns mirrored their predecessors', as reliance on particular types of donors was identical. In addition, campaign sophistication was consistent over time in the few cities where past and recent candidates' reliance on party and individual contributions varied.

Receiving substantial contributions from organizations, however, appeared related to campaign style. Fourteen recent candidates abandoned contributions from organizations, even though prior mayoral candidates in their cities had received them. Most of these candidates who turned their backs on—or were spurned by—organizations failed to expand the sophistication of mayoral campaigns in their particular cities. Only two used more sophisticated tactics than their predecessors had. Six used the same number, and another six incorporated fewer sophisticated tactics into their electoral efforts than prior mayoral candidates had. Meanwhile, thirteen recent candidates were the first in their respective cities to seek out substantial contributions from organizations. An opposite and even stronger pattern emerges for the campaign sophistication of these candidates. Of these candidates, none failed to fulfill expectations for sophisticated tactics created by prior mayoral candidates. Four used the same number of sophisticated tactics as their predecessors had, while nine increased the number of sophisticated tactics that had been used in their cities. Thus, when candidates refused or failed to attract donations from organizations, sophistication had at least a slight tendency to drop. Yet when organizational contributions first became important, sophistication levels were apt to increase.

Subtle Patterns Can Evoke Suspicions

These empirical observations indicate alterations in candidates' fundraising strategies cannot be described as revolutionary. Most mayoral candidates still rely heavily on small individual contributions, regardless of their adoption of advanced communication technology. Local candidates are not shifting the entire increased burden of campaign finance to special interests. The necessity of money in new-style campaigns, however, does appear to expand the role that organizations play in funding political campaigns. Admittedly, the relationship between organizational contributions is subtle. Yet the consequences of this pattern are compounded as political units become smaller. As in the national electorate, organized special interests capable of making substantial contributions beyond average citizens' capacities are present in smaller electorates. Unlike national politics, the efforts of special interests active in local political arenas are less apt to be counteracted by an opposing organization. Since new-style campaigns denigrate resources other than money and encourage candidates to rely on organizations for financial support, their presence in a smaller political unit creates the potential for unchallenged influence by a handful of local special interests. As the stories of mayoral campaigns in Albany illustrate, even subtle shifts in fundraising strategies can produce contributions with the potential to raise voters' suspicions of undue influence. It seems probable that robust contributions from a few well-known local organizations would make an even stronger impression on voters. If these types of contributions are publicized by opposing candidates or the media, they may have more dramatic implications on the electorate's perceptions than can be conveyed by this quantitative analysis.

SPECIAL INTEREST CONTRIBUTIONS IN DAYTON, OHIO   A striking example to illustrate this point comes from a competitive mayoral race in Dayton, Ohio, population 166,179. The 1997 election featured an incumbent, Republican Mike Turner, versus Democratic challenger Tony Capizzi. Both candidates raised enough funds to blanket the airwaves in the weeks prior to election day. Turner, whose total campaign budget was $177,860, spent nearly $110,000 on television commercials alone. Although his media campaign featured one negative radio ad, as the incumbent he dedicated his television spots to positive messages. Two emphasized successful programs implemented during his tenure in office, while a third showed off his "all-American family."[52] As the election neared, one editorial rejoiced, "Just two more days of flipping on the television to be greeted by Dayton mayor Mike Turner hugging and kissing his dark-haired little girls."[53] Meanwhile, Capizzi, whose total campaign budget was $82,554, combined efforts with the local Democratic Party to air $70,000 worth of television spots criticizing the mayor on several fronts. In particular, his efforts targeted African American radio stations and television channels to reach Democratic voters in the city's west side.[54]

When Capizzi, who was outspent nearly two-to-one, lost the race, the chair of the Montgomery County Democratic Party complained in the local paper, "The process has become driven by money, and that's really sad. . . . It's gotten to the point where it costs so much just to be competitive, and the person who raises the most money usually wins."[55] If this comment was not enough to damage average citizens' sense of political efficacy, the same newspaper article included a list of the candidates' biggest campaign contributions. Turner had received a series of large contributions from local business interests in the following amounts: $15,000, $7,500, $6,000, $6,000, and $5,000. The $15,000 contribution was the largest ever made to a local candidate in the city of Dayton. The article noted that Capizzi's fundraising relied on smaller individual contributions of about $100, but also reported two contributions from local unions for $5,000 and $4,100.[56] These amounts surely made the average citizens of Dayton question their ability to make meaningful contributions in future elections.

Consequences for Interactions between Candidates and Citizens

With encroaching campaign sophistication, average citizens are losing some of their access to local electoral processes. New-style campaigns make it more difficult for them to run for office and to provide meaningful contributions to favored candidates. Yet these two activities are not the only way that members of the electorate participate in political campaigns. The opportunity to interact with candidates personally is equally important. Meeting candidates enables voters to communicate their concerns and to influence candidates' positions, as well as to learn about their choices. In short, interaction empowers the electorate and provides the ability to hold public officials accountable. Nevertheless, new-style campaigns raise the concern that grassroots channels of communication will be abandoned in favor of more efficient, albeit impersonal, approaches. Candidates who adopt sophisticated campaign strategies may also be able to flood the local information environment with their own persuasive efforts and to dominate the messages received by the electorate. Finally, shifts in communication patterns caused by introducing new technologies might affect the content of candidate messages, thus altering the quality of politicians' rhetoric. Whether campaign sophistication affects the level of face-to-face contact that is occurring, the amount of information disseminated, or the type of messages conveyed needs to be assessed.

The Importance of Maintaining Direct Contact

Traditional campaign tactics that bring voters into direct contact with candidates or their volunteers have been praised for providing latent benefits to the political system.[57] Old-style campaign activities, such as giving speeches, attending neighborhood parties, or canvassing door-to-door, provide voters with the opportunity for personal involvement in the governing process. These activities enhance citizen involvement by encouraging voters to bring concerns to present and future officials and to engage in discussions about political issues. The exchanges "that occur between field workers, candidates, campaign staffs, and ordinary voters are an important part of the dialogue of democracy."[58] The communication technology of new-style campaigns helps candidates break the very barriers of time and space that make such personal dialogues necessary. Some side effects of new-style campaigns may have a positive result. Since candidates typically limit their time-consuming personal appeals to people who are registered, likely voters, the incorporation of communication technology into their campaign efforts would provide them with a time-efficient way to reach members of the electorate beyond this core of active voters. In this case, the addition of sophisticated tactics may help to improve the information environments of local elections, which are often dependent on campaign rhetoric, by increasing the overall quantity of campaign messages distributed. But such efficiency cannot replace the benefits provided by direct contact and discussion with candidates. Small political units, where direct contact with many voters is possible, provide candidates with the ideal opportunity to generate these latent benefits for the political system. Thus, the adoption of new-style campaigns could be cause for concern if local government candidates replace, rather than supplement, more traditional campaign activities.

In larger electoral districts, communication technology gained prominence as the number of party volunteers available to contact voters diminished. This coincidence raises concerns about the phenomenon of new-style local campaigns. If indirect contact through mailings and the electronic media replaced personal interactions between local politicians and their electorates, one of the simplest and most effective ways of linking citizens to their representatives would be lost.

Recall, however, that this particular side effect has not occurred in Albany, New York. The two most innovative mayoral candidates in the city's history, Carl Touhey and Jerry Jennings, both embraced traditional tactics providing face-to-face contact with the electorate. Despite Touhey's use of public opinion polls and television commercials, he literally wore out his walking shoes while canvassing door-to-door. Twenty-four years later, Jennings spent an unprecedented amount of money in order to incorporate advanced communication technology in his campaign. Yet he made every effort to meet with his constituents in person. These two aggressive candidates adopted new tactics because, like most candidates, they wanted to win. For the same reason, they did not abandon tried-and-true grassroots efforts that are so easy to implement in smaller districts.

PERSONAL CONTACT WITH VOTERS IS PRESERVED   Similarly, mayoral candidates in America's midsized cities still rely heavily on traditional tactics such as yard signs, speeches, literature drops, newspaper advertisements, and canvassing. As table 4.4 shows, the use of these five traditional tactics is actually positively related to new-style campaigns. The candidates who used at least two sophisticated tactics were slightly more apt to have used each of these five tactics than were their less-innovative counterparts. The percentage increase in their use of particular tactics ranged from 6 percent to 11 percent. Local candidates with sophisticated campaigns were more reliant on grassroots activities. At worst, they could be described as at least as active in pursuing personal contact with constituents as their more traditional counterparts were.

These findings suggest that local office seekers turn to both sophisticated and traditional tactics in contested races. Candidates adopt communication technology when they feel pressured to enhance their ability to persuade voters. At such times, candidates in local races are unlikely to abandon grassroots activities. These are more easily accomplished in smaller electoral districts, and personal contact with the candidate is one of the most persuasive weapons in a campaign's arsenal. Thus, local candidates use new-style activities to

Table 4.4   Sophisticated Candidates' Increase Grassroots Efforts

Traditional Tactic	% of Less Sophisticated Candidates Using Tactic	% of More Sophisticated Candidates Using Tactic	% Increase
Literature Drops	88	99	+11
Speeches	89	99	+10
Newspaper Ads	83	92	+ 9
Yard Signs	91	99	+ 8
Canvassing	80	86	+ 6

Source: 1998 interviews about the most recent mayoral candidates in midsized cities.

supplement, rather than to replace, traditional tactics. Instead of abandoning time-consuming, labor-intense efforts, they are adding new layers of sophisticated activities to their campaigns. Not only is the beneficial interaction between public officials and the electorate preserved, the overall number of messages disseminated surely increases. With the assistance of communication technology, candidate rhetoric will also reach a wider audience than the active voters typically contacted in grassroots efforts. By adopting sophisticated tactics, candidates may be improving the information environments of local government campaigns, as such races often receive limited coverage from the news media. Hence, this aspect of new-style local campaigns may provide positive side effects for democracy in America's localities.

The Importance of Balanced Rhetorical Contributions

Note, however, that the addition of sophisticated communication efforts to the local information environment would be beneficial only if both candidates used them. By its very nature, campaign rhetoric is subjective. It tells one candidate's side of the story and is intended to be persuasive. If only one candidate uses communication technology to increase the quantity of messages conveyed, the information environment would be biased in his or her favor. As one political observer notes, "A massive media campaign (particularly in congressional races where there is less free media coverage) can blot out the message of a candidate's opponent even where he [sic] has a strong grassroots organization."[59]

Moreover, the quality of information that voters receive from campaign rhetoric is enhanced when candidates react to opponents' platforms. Such interaction exposes voters to competing values and ideas and encourages them to critically evaluate solutions to social problems, rather than to simply accept pat answers. When emphasizing differences, candidates' rhetoric also underscores the notion that citizens have a choice and their vote matters. Yet candidates are not likely to defend their positions on controversial issues unless pushed to do so by an opponent. Instead, they will emphasize valence or "motherhood and apple pie" issues. As indicated by their nickname, such uncontroversial issues are nearly universally supported in the United States. In fact, political consultants often advise candidates to rely on valence issues precisely because they will not alienate any potential supporters.[60] Hence, the quality of campaign rhetoric is improved when candidates respond to one another, and when one candidate's messages do not dominate the information environment.

The structure of interviews with political reporters makes it difficult to assess whether opposing mayoral candidates were equally influential in shaping electoral information environments. Reporters were asked to indicate whether a tactic was used, not to evaluate the extent of its use. So, while both candidates in a race may have used television advertisements, one may have scraped enough money together for a last-minute blitz, whereas the other candidate may have broadcast a full array of television spots over several weeks. Yet the discrepancy in candidates' access to the financial resources implies that certain types of candidates will have more influence over political information provided to the voters.

A Biased Information Environment in Albany, New York

The 1997 mayoral race in Albany clearly illustrates the importance of such inequities. At first glance, Jerry Jennings's and Jack McEneny's campaign efforts may appear to be equally matched. Both candidates relied on almost all grassroots activities. Although Jennings had more time to canvass, McEneny and his volunteers made substantial efforts to meet individual voters. By the end of the campaign season, both candidates had also used a full array of sophisticated tactics, including public opinion polls, direct mail, radio advertisements, television commercials, and Internet sites. However, a more in-depth look at the race reveals that McEneny's efforts were overshadowed by Jennings's overwhelming presence on television.

With ample funds, Jennings chose to rely heavily on the pervasive medium of broadcast television. Throughout the race, he aired a series of three commercials to emphasize his campaign theme, which was "I Believe in Albany." His efforts were reminiscent of Ronald Reagan's "It's Morning Again in America" advertisement in 1984. They featured Jennings interacting with city residents, as well as softened images of the city's buildings, parks, and skyline, while emphasizing the mayor's successes. One focused on the money that Jennings's budgets had saved the city, and another extolled the city's summer jobs programs, which provides city youth with jobs. Finally, the third celebrated a recent decrease in Albany's violent crime rate. McEneny could not afford to air a television commercial until he altered his fundraising strategy near the end of the campaign. His single advertisement, which featured the candidate surrounded by a group of children, made no attempt to critique the incumbent's performance as mayor. Instead, it emphasized his long history of public service and his commitment to the city of Albany.

By the time the advertisement was aired, the overall tone of the race had been set. It was too late to force Jennings into interactions that would have required him to defend his administration. As a result, Jennings's message, which emphasized his accomplishments, dominated the most pervasive medium available and set the tone of the campaign. He was never forced to use his television time to discuss serious issues facing the city or how he would handle them. As one local political observer noted, "The question then becomes, has Jack McEneny given the voters sufficient cause not to vote for Jerry Jennings?"[61] He went on to claim that McEneny ran a "lousy" campaign because, "he's missed opportunity after opportunity to nail Jerry on the failings of the administration, from the crumbling of Central Avenue and the neighborhoods to what reassessment is going to really mean to at least a third of city residents."[62]

McEneny did attempt to publicize such criticisms in the more cost-efficient medium of radio. His campaign staff developed three radio advertisements. One featured a sarcastic female voice criticizing the mayor for claiming that he felt safe walking on any city street after dark. Another combined the same female voice with statements by the candidate chastising Jennings for failing to oppose the governor's plan to relocate thousands of state employees to another city. McEneny's third radio spot simulated a conversation between two Albany residents. McEneny's accomplishments were emphasized, whereas Jennings's reliance on large contributions was mentioned. In fact, Jennings aired a radio advertisement of his own in order to rebut several of these charges. Yet this interplay made little impression on local political pundits or on the Albany electorate. Radio reaches a smaller, more targeted audience than does broadcast television. Thus, McEneny's message was simply overpowered by the incumbent's pervasive blitz of television advertising. In previous years, McEneny's approach may have been more effective. Yet in 1997, Jennings's actions placed the mayoral debate in a different medium. McEneny's strained financial resources prevented him from buying television time in order to participate in that debate. The bulk of the arguments reaching the electorate and attracting media coverage presented Jerry Jennings's viewpoint and produced a biased information environment.

As the primary season came to a close, McEneny said, "My biggest problem has been a mayor who has refused . . . to participate in debates where I get to ask him questions and he gets to ask me questions. . . . I wish they would realize the mayor has gone out of his way to avoid any comparison with me."[63] Refusal to participate in debates is a common incumbent strategy that frustrates many challengers. Unfortunately, challengers cannot rely on debates or news coverage to carry their messages to the electorate. To be compared with the incumbent, they must develop and communicate their own rhetoric. In addition, they must do so in a way that prevents their message from being overshadowed. In short, if McEneny had been willing to raise more money, he could have forced Jennings to be compared with him by purchasing television airtime. By limiting contributions, McEneny also prevented his message from reaching the electorate.

SPENDING DISCREPANCIES PRODUCE BIAS   In an era of new-style campaigns, balanced information environments depend on both candidates' access to funds. Money is essential to disseminating additional messages through communication technology. It also purchases professional expertise to guarantee that the technology is used to achieve maximum impact. When candidates rely solely on grassroots activities, or perhaps even on simply less-advanced sophisticated tactics, to oppose a highly sophisticated opponent, they run the serious risk that their message will be overwhelmed. In this light, the spending discrepancies previously identified become even more troubling. Candidates with smaller budgets may be attempting to keep up with their opponents' use of sophisticated tactics. Without access to similar funds, however, their communication efforts and ability to compete will suffer in comparison.

The Importance of Quality Campaign Rhetoric

Although the quality of campaign rhetoric is less important in national and statewide races, where ample media coverage creates rich information environments, the paucity of such coverage in many local electoral races forces the electorate to rely on candidate advertising as a primary source of information. Yet opinions about the impact of communication technology on the quality of campaign rhetoric vary widely. Some suggest that sophisticated tactics inevitably result in more negative, deceptive, or manipulative messages. Obviously, increasing the number of messages disseminated to the electorate could be harmful to democracy if the electorate is alienated or manipulated by them. The ability to produce and disseminate messages quickly with communication technology has also been linked to increased negativity. Candidates now have the ability to respond rapidly to opponents' criticisms during a campaign by defending themselves or by making countercharges. As a result, technology may lead to a "punch, counterpunch" style of campaigning that was less possible in earlier eras.

Others, especially members of the consulting profession, have argued that the effect of communication technology in political campaigns has been overwhelmingly beneficial. While acknowledging that candidates sometimes rely on offensive, negative advertising, they note that these types of political charges have a long history in American politics. Moreover, today's critical advertisements are more likely to focus on legitimate subjects, such as missed votes or changed issue stands, rather than on personal attacks. Such advocates claim, "Smear tactics in American politics not only predate the development of the political consulting profession and negative advertising, but were considerably more slanderous in the days before television."[64]

Other observers of new-style political campaigns seem to have adopted a more moderate approach, suggesting that sophisticated communication tactics can have beneficial or harmful effects, depending on how they are used. This position is based on the argument that issues have never become political unless people held strong and often emotional opinions about them. Playing on such concerns to garner political support is not a new tactic. Similarly, subjective claims and negativity are not novelties in American political rhetoric.[65]

With all of these competing arguments, it is difficult to predict the effect of new-style campaigns on campaign rhetoric in local electoral districts. Whether the effect is beneficial or harmful may depend on the way individual candidates and their consultants decide to employ available technologies. The quality of local candidates' rhetoric cannot be assessed with data from either the mail survey of general consultants or the telephone interviews with political reporters, as these research tools were not designed to gather substantive accounts of candidates' communication efforts. Yet personal interviews with political actors in Albany yielded a striking contradiction of some critics' expectations.

Carl Touhey Takes the High Road

Carl Touhey's behavior in Albany's 1973 mayoral race provides evidence that diminished rhetoric is not inherently linked to new-style campaigns. Touhey had ample ammunition that he could have used to criticize the incumbent mayor, Erastus Corning. One did not need to dig too deeply to find shortcomings in both Corning's personal life and his performance as an elected official. Yet Touhey made the decision to avoid references to either in his campaign efforts.

First, according to his biographer, Corning was suspected of having a long-term affair with his former secretary, Dorothea "Polly" Noonan, who, rather than the mayor's wife, was his typical companion at political events. "From the outset of their lifelong relationship, Corning and Noonan were seen together around the Capitol, at political meetings, campaign dinners, Elks Club dances and committeeman strategy sessions."[66] These public appearances only fueled speculations about the couple's relationship. Regardless of whether the rumors were true, they were widely believed.[67] Touhey's comments about changes in campaign news coverage indicate that he was well aware of these suspicions. While being interviewed, he noted, "If he [Corning] were running today, Polly would be on the front page of the newspaper."[68] Yet despite Touhey's knowledge and his reliance on technology, the mayor's possible infidelity was never even considered a potential campaign issue.

Second, Touhey could have found more relevant fodder for negative advertisements from Corning's performance as mayor. During his tenure, Corning had been repeatedly investigated by the New York State Temporary Commission of Investigations for a series of offenses.[69] Furthermore, during the 1973 campaign season, he was required to testify at hearings to explore charges of corruption in the city's police department and improprieties in city purchasing practices.[70] Despite the urging of his campaign staff, Touhey refused to incorporate these charges into any of his communication efforts. He explicitly rejected radio and television scripts because they contained the line "the smell of corruption has hung over city hall for many years."[71] Touhey wanted to win by stressing the positive contributions he could make in city government, and he steadfastly rejected negative attacks on the mayor. After the campaign was over, his campaign manager told a reporter:

> There were some of us trying to get Carl to be tougher on Corning through the campaign, but he wouldn't do it. For instance, he wouldn't let us use the word "corruption" in any of our ads, and he wouldn't deal in innuendo. We had to be able to prove any charge we made before Carl would approve it.[72]

In explaining his refusal to personally criticize the mayor, Touhey said, "I probably should have. But it wasn't within me to do it. And you shouldn't do something you don't feel like doing."[73] The media firm handling Touhey's campaign produced two additional television commercials, exploiting charges faced by the current administration. One stressed the State Investigations Commission's claim that the city had lost parking meter revenues. Another, based on accusations of police corruption, featured a prostitute who explained that her business activities were protected by local politicians.[74] These commercials, however, were never used. According to a newspaper account, one advertising executive said, "I don't think Carl even saw those ads, his people said they would upset him too much."[75]

Instead of opting for these types of advertisements, Touhey chose to air a commercial intended to diminish citizens' fears of retribution from the machine. According to Touhey, Albany citizens wanted change, but most were afraid to show their support in public. One of his media advisers explained, for example, that many even believed that election workers loyal to the machine would be able to identify which candidates people voted for in the primary.[76] Obviously, such fears were detrimental to Touhey's, and to any other maverick candidate's, political ambitions. To address this belief, Touhey and his media advisers developed a television commercial that he can be proud of more than twenty years later. The advertisement featured a voting machine situated on a desolate hilltop in the nearby Adirondack Mountains. With the wind blowing fiercely, an actor walked into the machine and closed the curtain. A few seconds later, he opened the curtain and exited the machine. The script accompanying this simple act and breathtaking landscape reassured viewers that they would be equally isolated when casting their votes for mayor and encouraged them to "vote their conscience."[77]

Despite the recommendations of his advisers, Touhey chose to reject advertising that could be perceived in any way as negative. His efforts could have withstood the scrutiny of the most severe critics of political advertising. Not only were commercials appealing to voters' base emotions avoided, Touhey even refused to air charges that many would argue were legitimate criticisms of the mayor's performance in office. For example, one might legitimately believe that repeated inquiries by the State Investigations Commission warranted the claim that "the smell of corruption has hung over city hall for many years." Regardless, Touhey drew the line at advertising that he believed to be inappropriate. Moreover, he went beyond simply refraining from criticisms. Granted, Touhey benefited from the message communicated to the electorate in the voting machine advertisement. He was motivated at least in part by self-interest. Yet the advertisement encouraged citizens to exercise their right to choose and can only be described as positive political rhetoric.

Two possible explanations for Touhey's decisions exist. First, Touhey's decisions may have been related to the relatively small size of the Albany electorate. Touhey and Mayor Corning moved in the same social circles. They were both members of the exclusive Fort Orange Club and even served on some of the same boards of directors. Touhey acknowledged that he knew the mayor very well, while one of his media advisers even claimed the two were friends.[78] By all accounts, they maintained a cordial relationship even throughout the campaign. Touhey, for example, relayed a story of an interaction during a meeting of the board of the National Commercial Bank & Trust, on which both men served. Touhey had a hole in his shoe from canvassing, and the director, comparing Touhey to Adlai Stevenson, pointed it out. Touhey laughed and recalled that Corning then muttered, "He [Stevenson] didn't get elected either."[79] This familiarity between opponents, which is obviously more likely to occur in smaller communities, may have suppressed any inclination Touhey had to attack the mayor. Proximity to his friends and family could have been a similar deterrent. Touhey owned several businesses in and around the city, and he had no intention of leaving. Whether he won or lost, he still had to face his friends, neighbors, and business associates on a daily basis. Perhaps he did not want to be identified for the rest of his life as the man whose advertising shocked the city. Consequently, local candidates might be inclined to temper their rhetoric, regardless of the technology used, in order to preserve their standing in their hometown communities.

On the other hand, Touhey may simply have been a unique candidate who was able to overcome the temptation to use the electronic media to air negative or half-true charges. Typical candidates' desires to win at all costs may make such options more palatable to them. Touhey did not have this type of drive, as he explained, "This [the election] wasn't life or death to me."[80] He had entered the race knowing that his chances of winning were slim. When interviewed, he acknowledged that the odds of his success were 100 to 1 and jokingly said, "If I had been elected, I would have called for a re-count."[81]

OTHER LOCAL CANDIDATES GO NEGATIVE   Stories of campaigns in other localities suggest that more ambitious politicians are more willing to go negative. In the 1999 mayoral race in Bradenton, Florida, for example, the incumbent mayor Bill Evers struck out at his challenger during a televised debate. Drawing gasps from the audience, Evers accused Wayne Poston of being the "handpicked puppet" of a "few rich, greedy people who want to take over the city."[82] Later in the campaign, Evers mailed a flier that accused Poston of supporting the death penalty. The flier featured an elderly woman peeking out from behind a locked door. The red-lettered caption read: "She didn't deserve to die. Her killer does. Wayne Poston would let him live."[83] The flier went on to explain that the *Bradenton Herald* had editorialized against the death penalty during Poston's tenure as editor and concluded that Poston was "just like all the other liberals with more concern for the criminals than the victims and their families."[84]

Meanwhile, two years earlier in Dayton, Ohio, the chair of the Montgomery County Republican Party mailed a letter to raise funds for incumbent mayor Mike Turner that personally attacked challenger Tony Capizzi. It read: "All over the Miami Valley, here's what people tell me. . . . Tony Capizzi is not the person we want representing us. He's rude. He's arrogant. He's only interested in promoting himself."[85]

These stories make it clear that Carl Touhey is only one of the multitude of local candidates who have run for office in the United States. Yet his story clearly illustrates that the quality of political rhetoric ultimately depends on the candidate, rather than on the medium used to communicate it. His advertising decisions show that communication technology can be used to the electorate's benefit and at least raise speculation that diminished political rhetoric may be less of a concern in local electoral arenas.

Conclusion

A blanket statement about the effect of encroaching campaign sophistication cannot be derived from the evidence presented throughout this chapter. Describing it as either entirely beneficial or detrimental to democracy in U.S. localities would be misleading. The true effects are far more nuanced. The adoption of communication technology does not encourage local government candidates to abandon tried-and-true grassroots activities. Rather than replacing personal interaction with voters, sophisticated tactics are used to increase the overall amount of political rhetoric disseminated. Such efforts have the potential not only to improve local information environments, but to expand the circle of citizens receiving political information beyond a core of active, registered voters. Moreover, Carl Touhey's advertising decisions lead to speculation that community forces such as familiarity can help to preserve the quality of political rhetoric, regardless of the communication channels that local government candidates rely upon.

On the other hand, the trend toward sophistication does increase the financial burden of running for office, as new-style campaigns require money to purchase technology and expertise. The negative consequences of increasing campaign budgets are threefold. First, such increases enhance the advantages enjoyed by both incumbents and candidates with higher social-class standing. They raise more money than other types of candidates do and surely find the prospect of running a new-style campaign less intimidating as a result. Fewer potential candidates with lower socioeconomic status may be willing to run for office. Their failure to run for office will eventually affect the types of people serving in local, as well as state and national, governments, and elected officials will share fewer demographic characteristics with their constituents. Second, some candidates respond to increased financial needs by bolstering their reliance on funds from organizations, but this practice denigrates average citizens' abilities to make meaningful campaign contributions. Third, spending inequities enable incumbents and higher-class candidates to overwhelm opponents' communication efforts and to dominate local information environments.

The positive contributions of encroaching sophistication cannot erase the serious impact of these troubling side effects. Thus, some may react to these findings by prescribing a return to traditional campaigns for local government offices. This recommendation would be difficult to achieve because, for the reasons described in chapter 3, the trend appears to be both progressive and irreversible. Moreover, this remedy would also require abandoning new-style campaigns' contributions to local democracy. Hence, the feasibility of reforms to ameliorate detrimental effects, while preserving beneficial ones, is the topic of the concluding chapter.

Notes

1. Dennis Schrader, Howard County executive candidate, telephone interview by J. Cherie Strachan. Tape recording, October 2001.
2. Gady A. Epstein, "Robey Launches Political TV Ads," *The Baltimore Sun,* 1 September 1998, 1(A).
3. Gady A. Epstein, "Schrader, Robey Keep Fund Raising All in the Family," *The Baltimore Sun,* 25 October 1998, 1 (B); and Vicky Goodman, Robey campaign adviser, telephone interview by J. Cherie Strachan. Tape recording, October 2001.
4. Goodman interview.
5. Edward Lee, "Race Becomes Run for Money," *The Baltimore Sun,* 20 October 1998, 1(B).
6. As quoted by Jay Jochnowitz, "Sizing Up the Strategy in the Mayor's Race," *Times Union* (Albany, N.Y.), 18 July 1993, 3(C).
7. Rachel McEneny, McEneny campaign manager, interview by J. Cherie Strachan. Tape recording, Albany, N.Y., April 1998.
8. As quoted by Kate Gurnett and Jay Jochnowitz, "It's All Down to the Count," *Times Union* (Albany, N.Y.), 6 September 1997, 1(A) and 4(A).
9. "Woulda Shoulda Coulda," *Metroland* (Albany, N.Y.), 18–25 September 1997, 9.
10. As quoted by Jay Jochnowitz, "It's Jennings, and It's a Landslide," *Times Union* (Albany, N.Y.), 10 September 1997, 5(A).
11. As quoted in "Woulda Shoulda Coulda," 9.
12. Martha Modeen, "Mayoral Candidate Is Disqualified," *The News Tribune* (Tacoma, Wash.), South Sound Section, 10 August 2001, 4(B).
13. Martha Modeen, "Five Seek Top City Job in Low-Budget Effort," *The News Tribune* (Tacoma, Wash.), South Sound Section, 10 September 2001, 1(A); and Martha Modeen, "Looks Like Baarsma or Moss," *The News Tribune* (Tacoma, Wash.), South Sound Section, 19 September 2000, 11(A).
14. Modeen, "Five Seek Top City Job," 1(A); and Martha Modeen, "Candidates Kick Off Campaigns," *The News Tribune* (Tacoma, Wash.), South Sound Section, 3 May 2001, 1(B).
15. Everett M. Rogers, *Diffusion of Innovations,* 3rd ed. (New York: Free Press, 1983), 263.
16. In addition, several reporters qualified the use of communication technology by unopposed incumbents who used the campaign season not to promote their own candidacies, but to gain influence over the city council by attempting to sway public support in favor of a pet project or policy.
17. Rather than the interviewer providing them with a list of criteria, such as income or education levels, reporters were simply asked to estimate each candidate's socioeconomic status. Given Americans' tendency to associate most people with the middle class, however, reporters' perceptions may have underestimated the number of upper-class mayoral candidates.
18. R. Darcy, Susan Welch, and Janet Clark, *Women, Elections and Representation* (Lincoln: University of Nebraska Press, 1994).

19. See Sandy L. Maisel, "The Incumbency Advantage," in *Money Elections and Democracy: Reforming Congressional Campaign Finance,* ed. Margaret Latus Nugent and John R. Johannes (Boulder, Colo: Westview, 1990), 119–41; Frank J. Sorauf, *Money in American Elections* (Boston: Scott, Foresman and Company, 1988); and Frank J. Sorauf, "Competition, Contributions, and Money in 1992," in *Campaigns and Elections American Style,* ed. James A. Thurber and Candice J. Nelson (Boulder, Colo.: Westview, 1995), 78–83.

20. Daniel M. Shea, *Campaign Craft: The Strategies, Tactics and Art of Political Campaign Management* (Westport, Conn.: Praeger, 1996), 183.

21. Ann Beaudry and Bob Schaeffer, *Winning Local and State Elections: The Guide to Organizing Your Campaign* (New York: Free Press, 1986), 164.

22. Obtaining spending information from local campaign finance filing offices is usually difficult even when the researcher can appear in person. Gathering it from such offices in cities scattered across the country is next to impossible. Since candidate spending is a standard news story, most reporters recalled or had access to this information.

23. Jay Jochnowitz and Tom Precious, "McCall Gets Some Wall Street Friends to Help Out Jennings," *Times Union* (Albany, N.Y.), 29 October 1993, 1(A) and 8(A).

24. Jochnowitz and Precious, "McCall Gets Some Wall Street Friends," 1(A) and 8(A).

25. Carl Touhey, Albany mayoral candidate, interview by J. Cherie Strachan. Tape recording, Albany, N.Y., May 1998.

26. Paul Grondahl, *Mayor Corning: Albany Icon, Albany Enigma* (Albany, N.Y.: Washington Park Press, 1997), 324–25.

27. Grondahl, *Mayor Corning,* 324–25.

28. Carol DeMare, "Bytner 'Sideshow' Bane of Corning and Touhey," *Times Union* (Albany, N.Y.), 11 October 1973, 3.

29. Touhey interview; and Grondahl, *Mayor Corning,* 325.

30. John McLoughlin, "$3,500 Question: Is Corning Popular?" *Times Union* (Albany, N.Y.), 31 May 1973, 3; and Joe Picchi, "Quayle Poll Shows Touhey Leading," *Times Union* (Albany, N.Y.), 16 October 1973, 3.

31. Touhey interview.

32. Jay Jochnowitz, "Alderman St. John Sidesteps Mayoral Run," *Times Union* (Albany, N.Y.), 8 June 1993, 1(B).

33. Emily Lemke, Cherokee County chair, telephone interview by J. Cherie Strachan. Tape recording, September 2001.

34. D. L. Bennett, "An Election Report, Lathem Funding Sets County Record," *Atlanta Journal Constitution,* 16 July 1998, 4(JQ).

35. D. L. Bennett, "An Election Report," 4(JQ).

36. Lemke interview.

37. Lemke interview.

38. "Expense of Local Political Races Is Outrageous," *Las Vegas Review Journal,* 9 September 2000, 14(B).

39. As quoted by Berny Morson, "School Candidates in Spending Spiral," *Rocky Mountain News* (Denver, Colo.), 18 October 1993, 17(A).

40. As quoted by Morson, "School Candidates in Spending Spiral," 17(A).

41. Shea, *Campaign Craft*, 180.

42. James Madison, "Federalist #10," *The Federalist Papers* (New York: Penguin, 1961), 77–84.

43. Jochnowitz, "Alderman St. John," 8(A).

44. Michael McKeon, "Jennings Jabs at Joyce over $50,000 Fund-Raiser," *Times Union* (Albany, N.Y.), 3 April 1993, 1(B).

45. Fred LeBrun, "The Harold and Gerald Show, Yawn," *Times Union* (Albany, N.Y.), 7 September 1993, 1(B).

46. As quoted by Jochnowitz and Precious, "McCall Gets Some Wall Street Friends to Help Out Jennings," 1(A) and 8(A).

47. Jochnowitz and Precious, "McCall Gets Some Wall Street Friends to Help Out Jennings," 1(A) and 8(A).

48. Kate Gurnett and Jay Jochnowitz, "It's All Down to the Count," *Times Union* (Albany, N.Y.), 6 September 1997, 1(A) and 4(A).

49. McEneny interview.

50. This information was obtained from campaign finance reports filed with the Albany County Board of Elections.

51. Seventy-six reporters were familiar with the activities of prior mayoral candidates in their respective cities, so comparisons to past races could be made for 154 of the 217 most recent mayoral candidates.

52. David Mendell, "Mayor's Office Was Costly," *Dayton Daily News*, 13 December 1997, 1(B).

53. David Mendell, "Race-Closing Pitches Made," *Dayton Daily News*, 2 November 1997, 1(B).

54. Mendell, "Mayor's Office Was Costly, " 1(B); and Mendell, "Race-Closing Pitches Made, " 1(B).

55. As quoted by Mendell, "Mayor's Office Was Costly," 1(B).

56. Mendell, "Mayor's Office Was Costly," 1(B).

57. Paul Herrnson, "Field Work, Political Parties, and Volunteerism," in *Campaigns and Elections American Style*, ed. James A. Thurber and Candice J. Nelson (Boulder, Colo.: Westview, 1995), 160.

58. Herrnson, "Field Work, Political Parties, and Volunteerism," 160.

59. Frank I. Luntz, *Candidates, Consultants and Campaigns* (New York: Basic, 1988), 222.

60. Shea, *Campaign Craft*, 151.

61. Fred LeBrun, "McEneny Refuses to Give Up," *Times Union* (Albany, N.Y.), 6 September 1997, 1(B).

62. LeBrun, "McEneny Refuses," 1(B)

63. As quoted by Tim O'Brien, "Their Final Goal Is a Win Tuesday, " *Times Union* (Albany, N.Y.), 7 September 1997, 1(D) and 6(D).

64. Luntz, *Candidates, Consultants and Campaigns*, 228.

65. Lynda Lee Kaid, "Ethical Dimensions of Political Advertising," in *Ethical Dimensions of Political Communication*, ed. Robert Denton (New York: Praeger, 1991), 145–65.

66. Grondahl, *Mayor Corning*, 141.

67. Grondahl, *Mayor Corning*, 141–51.

68. Touhey interview.

69. Grondahl, *Mayor Corning*, 245–53.

70. Grondahl, *Mayor Corning*, 325.

71. John McLoughlin, "Touhey, Anatomy of an 'Almost' Win," *Times Union* (Albany, N.Y.), 11 November 1973, 1(E).

72. McLoughlin, "Touhey, Anatomy of an 'Almost' Win," 1(E).

73. Touhey interview.

74. McLoughlin, "Touhey, Anatomy of an 'Almost' Win," 1(E).

75. As quoted by McLoughlin, "Touhey, Anatomy of an 'Almost' Win" 1(E).

76. Noel "Bud" Johnson, Touhey campaign adviser, interview by J. Cherie Strachan. Tape recording, Troy, N.Y., May 1998.

77. Johnson interview.

78. Johnson interview; and Touhey interview.

79. Touhey interview; and Grondahl, *Mayor Corning*, 324.

80. Touhey interview.

81. Touhey interview.

82. As quoted by Matthew Henry, "Candidates Exchange Jabs in Debate," *Sarasota Herald Tribune*, Manatee Edition, 26 October 1999, 1(B).

83. "Bradenton's Mudslinging Mayor," *Sarasota Herald Tribune*, Manatee Edition, 22 November 1999, 1(A).

84. "Bradenton's Mudslinging Mayor," 1(A).

85. As cited in "Jacobsen Pitch Is the Thing People Hate," *Dayton Daily News*, 3 October 1997, 14(A).

Electoral Reform from the Grass Roots

The Function of Elections in Representative Democracy

Elections were first established in the American colonies to serve the purposes of democracy. Throughout U.S. history, as democratic sentiment expanded, so did reliance on elections as the preferred mechanism for selecting public officials. Hence, elections' raison d'être, the sole purpose behind their existence, is to enhance the citizenry's control over agents of their government.

As the years passed, a complex body of law outlining procedures to be followed in order to carry out elections has been enacted. Election law has moved far beyond merely determining the time and place for voters to cast their ballots. Reforms have always been couched in the language of democracy. For example, secret ballots were enacted to ensure that voters felt free to follow their consciences, registration requirements were put in place to suppress voter fraud, and limits on large campaign contributions were established to prevent elected officers from being bribed to overlook the public's best interest.

However, attempts to learn about U.S. elections merely by reading statute books would be misguided. While such an effort would provide details about the legal framework of elections, it would overlook the plethora of activities occurring during campaigns for public office. Those who participate in these activities include candidates, political parties, organized interest groups, and, of course, individual voters. One need only observe these actors' campaign practices for a short time to realize that they have their own agendas, which do not always correspond to democratic concerns. Although the practices of participants in the electoral process must fall within specified regulations, their efforts can still undermine democracy. Candidates enter electoral arenas with the goal of winning and may attempt to suppress competition in order to succeed. Incumbents, for example, often build huge war chests of funds to ward off potential challengers. Yet without incumbents facing strong competition, voters are denied the opportunity to reject them. Political parties have a similar agenda for winning elections. Extreme examples of their suppression of competition and its effect on accountability can be found in the party machines that at one time dominated city and state politics. Organized interest groups participate in elections to achieve influence over their particular policy concerns. To accomplish this task, they often make large campaign contributions, sometimes even to both candidates in a close race. This practice provides them with influence beyond their numbers in the electorate and undermines the ability of average citizens to hold elected officers accountable. Finally, accounts even exist of voters who abandon their opportunity to help elect public officers by selling their votes for monetary gain. In short, a schism often exists between the reason why elections exist and the way that they are used.

When such practices become customary, the electoral process is compromised. To return it to its original purpose, reforms updating electoral statutes and regulations must be adopted. Note, however, that the need for reform is never permanently eliminated, as campaign practices are dynamic. They exist within American society and reflect the changes occurring there. As soon as reforms are enacted to address one problem, changing circumstances allow political actors to devise new practices to pursue their own agendas, such as suppressing competition or pursuing undue influence. Hence, the long-term health of U.S. electoral processes depends upon willingness to reform them.

Evidence of the Need for Reform

Evidence presented throughout this work has outlined every step in this cycle of changing campaign practices, except for the adoption of effective reforms. Advancements in the field of communications initiated changes in the way that candidates campaign for office. Improvements in production processes resulted in the decreased cost of communication technology. While more affordable prices brought sophisticated campaign tactics into local government candidates' price ranges, it also enabled more people to enter the profession of political consulting. For example, the decreased cost of computers, which are a prerequisite for many consulting specialties, reduced the start-up cost of opening a consulting business and expanded the pool of available expert assistance. In addition, further technological development made it possible to use sophisticated tactics to target smaller groups of voters. Local candidates responded to these changes by incorporating elements of new-style campaign activities into their electoral efforts. As of 1998 local government candidates, ranging from county executives to school board members, had turned to the expertise of a general political consultant. In addition, 69 percent of the most recent mayoral candidates in U.S. midsized cities relied on at least two sophisticated tactics, and 64 percent hired one or more campaign professionals.

Candidates altered their campaign practices because sophisticated tactics helped them to pursue their agenda of winning elections. Some first turned to sophisticated tactics to gain a competitive edge over opponents in close races. The resulting contact between future candidates and political consultants encouraged more innovation. Finally, in many midsized cities, sophisticated tactics have become expected, and their presence is used by both reporters and voters to identify serious office seekers.

While serving candidates' agenda of winning, these new campaign practices have diminished the original purpose for undertaking elections because they hinder citizens' abilities to hold elected officials accountable. New-style campaigns' emphasis on financial resources has enhanced the advantages enjoyed by incumbents and upper-class candidates who have less difficulty amassing resources. As a result, these candidates are able to dominate local information environments during campaigns when they face less-advantaged opponents. Challengers and working-class candidates who persist in running for elected office find it difficult to establish themselves as serious candidates, and competition, so essential to providing voters with a choice, suffers. In addition, when candidates from lower socioeconomic backgrounds lose access to elected offices, either because they are apt to lose or because they are intimidated out of running, the diversity of officeholders in local, as well as state and national, governments is compromised. In short, the socioeconomic characteristics of officeholders look even less like those of the people they represent. Finally, the increased financial need created by new-style campaigns provides special interests, which pursue their own agenda in elections, with the opportunity to increase their influence at the expense of other actors. To return elections to their original purpose of accountability, reforms that take these new campaign practices into account must be undertaken.

Some critics might believe that a more appropriate reaction would be to avoid these problems altogether by simply abolishing new-style campaigns at the local level. Gaining local candidates' cooperation in such an effort, however, would be next to impossible. Candidates turn to communication technology because it enhances their chances of winning. The only effective check on local adoption of new-style campaigns would be rejection by the voters. Yet given the ease with which expectations about appropriate campaign tactics are altered, critics should not hold their breath waiting for the electorate to spurn candidates who rely on sophisticated electoral tactics. Moreover, such a drastic remedy would also require abandoning campaign sophistication's potential to improve local information environments and to spread political information beyond the core of active voters. To be effective, reform efforts must acknowledge the permanency of new-style local campaigns, while addressing their negative consequences for local democracy.

Note, however, that while the problems caused by campaign sophistication are particularly troubling for local electoral processes, they are by no
means unique. Similar concerns have plagued national and state electoral arenas as new-style campaigns became entrenched there. Consequently, to begin
developing remedies, local government reformers need not start from
scratch. One of the benefits of a federal system is the ability to imitate and
expand upon successful policies and practices enacted elsewhere within the
same political system. Insight can be gained by reviewing prior efforts,
enacted by both larger and smaller political units, to address the problems
created by campaign sophistication.

Reducing Undue Influence

When new-style campaigns, along with their emphasis on spending ability,
came to dominate presidential efforts, renewed concerns over appropriate
fundraising strategies were not far behind. In the 1970s, Congress enacted
comprehensive legislation intended to prevent undue influence from large
contributors. Original concerns over large contributions emphasized the fear
that public officials would be bribed to overlook the interests of their constituents. Obviously, government authority cannot serve the public when it is
for sale to the highest bidder. Yet as new-style campaigns became entrenched,
the ability to communicate persuasive information became more strongly
linked to the resource of money. Consequently, concerns over large contributions extended to include their effect on average citizens' abilities to influence election outcomes. Inequalities in the electoral process make bribery
unnecessary. If the wealthy can control which candidates win elections in the
first place, their particular interests will be favored automatically. "When citizens believe, rightly or wrongly, that their representatives are acting to further particular private interests, rather than the public interest, their support
for the regime declines."[1]

Concerns over such inequalities have been repeatedly voiced in the
national political arena. In 1993, for example, President Bill Clinton encouraged people "to resolve to reform our politics so that power and privilege no
longer shout down the voice of the people."[2] But campaign finance reforms
were not enacted during his tenure in office. Senator John McCain (R-AZ)
highlighted the need for reform during his unsuccessful bid for the Republican presidential nomination. Even after his loss, he used his celebrity status
and position within the Senate to keep the issue of campaign finance reform
on the agenda. Eventually, the Bipartisan Campaign Reform Act emerged
from both houses of Congress and was signed into law by President George
W. Bush in March 2002. The law, several aspects of which are currently being
challenged in federal court, is the first major attempt to reform federal cam-

paign practices in over twenty-five years. In that interim, many U.S. states and localities were far more active in pursuing electoral reform.

Similar Concerns Emerge in Albany, New York

Since local government candidates have begun imitating the fundraising strategies of their state and national counterparts, similar concerns over undue influence have been raised in smaller electoral districts across the country. In fact, the issue received considerable attention in Albany after the mayor's record-setting expenditure of over $400,000 in the 1997 race. A local political commentator wrote a blistering column calling for reform. His comments, quoted here, are a familiar refrain, but one more often directed toward state and national politics. He wrote:

> Have we all lost our minds or what? If we know anything from watching modern democracy, it's that most political contributors are investors. Money donated to campaigns has a disturbing tendency to make its way back to contributors—and with hefty interest—in the form of public spending in one way, shape or form. When we permit politicians to spend such huge sums on campaigns, it ends up costing us all money sooner or later.[3]

The commentator called for a local ordinance limiting citywide candidates' expenditures to $200,000 and countywide candidates to $400,000. He concluded: "You can argue about how to frame such a law. You can even argue about the spending limit. But nobody can argue convincingly anymore that a limit isn't needed."[4]

The Feasibility of Spending Limits

City officials attempting to address concerns over campaign finances with such an ordinance risk having their efforts stymied in the courts. While political reporters and even the general public might see a need for them, limits on the amount of money candidates can spend on their campaigns have been viewed as protected by the First Amendment, unless tied to voluntary acceptance of public financing, since the Supreme Court decided the landmark campaign finance case of *Buckley v. Valeo* in 1976. In its opinion, the Court explicitly equated campaign spending with political speech by claiming, "virtually every means of communicating ideas in today's mass society requires the expenditure of money."[5] Hence, the Court determined that many provisions of the federal law threatened candidates' free speech rights and therefore could not be upheld unless they served the compelling government interest of preventing actual or perceived bribery.[6] The notion that the state had a legitimate interest in equalizing citizens' influence was explicitly rejected. The Court noted: "The concept that government may restrict the speech of some elements in society in order to enhance the relative voice of others is wholly foreign to the First Amendment."[7] Moreover, the Court remained steadfast to this interpretation in ensuing cases over the next two decades.[8]

Some communities have responded to concerns by ignoring *Buckley v. Valeo* and enacting unconstitutional spending limits. One example can be found in the town of Crested Butte, Colorado, population 1,529. In 1995, a candidate for city council evoked town officials' concerns by spending more than $500. As a result, the town council drafted a referendum setting campaign spending limits at $200 per election, indexed annually at 3 percent for inflation, for town offices. It passed with an overwhelming 79 percent of the vote.[9] Despite this apparent success story, it is important to note that such restrictions are unconstitutional and will remain on the books only until they are challenged.

ORDINANCES CHALLENGED IN CINCINNATI, OHIO, AND ALBU-QUERQUE, NEW MEXICO   Such was the fate of expenditure limits enacted in the city of Cincinnati, population 331,285. Campaign spending by municipal candidates in Cincinnati had increased 482 percent between 1989 and 1995, from an average of $75,000 to $362,000. In response, a new ordinance restricted spending to three times the salary of the position sought. As a result, city council candidates were limited to $140,000 per election cycle. These limits were challenged by unsuccessful city council candidates in federal court. In its defense, the city of Cincinnati presented findings of a study commissioned by the Center for Responsive Politics, which concluded that increased spending had increased the influence of large campaign donors and relegated small donors to the role of marginal players in local electoral politics. In addition, a poll conducted by Deardoff/The Media Company documented city residents' concerns over local candidates' spending. Hence, the city argued that it had a compelling interest in controlling rising costs to reduce the amount of time candidates spend fundraising, to stem the erosion of public trust, and to eliminate the advantages of wealth. This reasoning was rejected and the ordinance deemed a violation of First Amendment rights because it was not narrowly tailored to prevent actual or perceived corruption.[10]

Even in communities with a long-term support of such limits, it only takes a single disgruntled candidate to launch such a challenge. Recent events in Albuquerque, New Mexico, population 448,607, illustrate that even towns where such restrictions have been part of a community's political history risk being taken to court. Albuquerque's city charter has included just such a restriction, capping municipal candidates' spending to the salary of the position sought, in its city charter since 1974. A member of the committee responsible for revising the charter explained that its purpose was "to equalize the playing field so that anybody could run if they had enough support in the community, whether they were rich or they were poor, (so) people couldn't just buy elections."[11] Martin Chavez won the city's mayoral election in 1993 and used the position as a stepping-stone to win the Democratic gubernatorial nomination in 1998. He attributed his success to the spending limits, noting that without them he "probably would have gotten outspent and come in third."[12] He also lamented the shift in his activities after leaving Albuquerque to run for governor. "Before, I was shaking hands and talking to people; I was addressing any forum that would have me. Now, 40 percent of my time is raising money," he said.[13]

Anecdotal evidence from Albuquerque's long experiment with expenditure limits suggests that these may have beneficial effects beyond eliminating undue influence. Incumbent mayors have had difficulty winning re-election since the law was enacted, with four going down in defeat.[14] Some claim that the competition resulted from a leveled playing field. One city council member, a special education teacher earning $36,000 a year, claimed, "I'm not independently wealthy, and I was on equal footing with everyone."[15] Yet Albuquerque's experiment with expenditure limits appears to be drawing to a close. In 1997, a mayoral candidate sought an injunction allowing candidates to exceed the cap. (Note, as spending increased in that race, voter turnout dropped, from 43 percent in 1993 down to 33 percent in 1997.[16]) The restrictions remained on the books as the candidate lost the election and dropped his suit, but another injunction has since been filed, and the limits are not currently enforced.[17]

Since the courts' opposition to spending limits appears unshaken, those developing local campaign finance policies would be advised to look for a more viable long-term solution, unless they intend to tie their limits to candidates' acceptance of public funding. Interest in establishing public financing for state candidates was renewed in the mid-1990s, particularly in the states of Maine, Vermont, and Nebraska.[18] Several cities have also recently turned to public financing in order to establish constitutional spending limits; these include New York City; Los Angeles; Long Beach, California; and Austin, Texas.[19] Maintaining such programs can be difficult. Problems include weakening financial bases, declining levels of public support, and difficulty securing all candidates' voluntary participation. In addition, it should be clearly noted that public funding programs may help alleviate candidates' fundraising burdens and level the playing field, but they do not automatically discourage sophisticated electoral efforts.

The Feasibility of Gaining Voluntary Cooperation

Another approach to restraining spending, without the accompanying complexity of public financing, is to enact voluntary spending limits and to discourage candidates from violating them. In some localities, this task is adopted by citizen organizations, which agree on appropriate spending limits for their communities. They take responsibility for asking candidates to comply and for publicizing the names of those who overspend. This solution relies on the enforcement mechanism of public pressure, which may not be enough to deter candidates who believe that they need to adopt sophisticated campaigns. Another problem with such solutions is that they rely on the continued vigilance of citizen organizations and the willingness of local media outlets to cover their complaints. Such citizen organizations were at one time active in Chapel Hill, North Carolina, population 48,715, and Boulder, Colorado, population 94,673. Both have since adopted enforceable legal reforms. Boulder adopted public financing and accompanying spending limits in 1999.[20] Meanwhile, Chapel Hill has a $200 limit on contributions to municipal candidates and requires full disclosure of all donations in excess of $20.[21]

As a result, some municipalities include incentives to cooperate with "voluntary" spending limits in city ordinances. Richland, Washington, population 38,708, established such limits, requiring the city clerk to publish newspaper advertisements identifying candidates who exceed them. Such advertisements are to be published weekly, from the time that limits are exceeded throughout the remainder of the election.[22]

CREATIVE COMPLIANCE INCENTIVES OVERTURNED IN MISSOURI Reformers should note, however, that the courts have already aborted similar creative attempts to limit campaign expenditures. A Missouri law attempted to enhance the importance of individual contributions by penalizing candidates who refused to comply with so-called voluntary spending limits. The law prohibited noncomplying candidates from accepting contributions from any source other than individuals. It also required them to file daily disclosure reports after exceeding the state-recommended expenditure limits. The law was overturned in federal court for imposing limits on political speech without serving the only acceptable compelling state interest, the prevention of bribery.[23]

The Feasibility of Low Contribution Limits

Other attempts to restrain the influence of wealthy interests have placed extremely low limits on the size of the contributions that candidates are allowed to accept. Fort Collins, Colorado, population 118,652, lowered the amount of contributions to city candidates from $100 to $50 in 1986, in order to combat corruption or the appearance of corruption in the local political process. These limits have since been raised to $75 for city council candidates and to $100 for mayoral candidates.[24] Another approach to restricting the size of contributions was taken in Westminster, Colorado, population 100,094. In a 1996 referendum, an overwhelming 70 percent of the city's voters enacted a conflict of interest ordinance. The regulation prohibits a member of the city council from voting on an issue affecting anyone who contributed more than $100 to the council member's campaign. According to city officials, city contractors and developers are now far less apt to make contributions exceeding $100.[25]

LOW CONTRIBUTIONS LIMITS OVERTURNED IN MISSOURI AND MINNESOTA   Again, such regulations are subject to judicial scrutiny if challenged, and initial decisions in such cases suggested that low limits would be overruled. The 1976 *Buckley* Court refused to overturn congressional limits on large contributions to federal candidates, in amounts of $1,000 from individuals and $5,000 from political action committees, because such restraints helped to prevent the appearance of bribery. Yet the justices also anticipated the possibility of more drastic limits and noted that these would be unconstitutional if "the limitations prevented candidates and political committees from amassing the resources necessary for effective advocacy."[26] Despite this precedent set for federal candidates, a Missouri ballot initiative, sponsored by the Association of Community Organizations for Reform Now (ACORN), called for limits on donations to state and local candidates. The initiative, which was approved in 1995 by an overwhelming 74 percent of the state's voters, limited contributions to $100 per election to candidates in districts with a population of less than 100,000; to $200 per election in districts with a population of greater than 100,000; and to $300 per election for statewide candidates.[27] In addition to limiting the influence of wealthy contributors, ACORN's agenda included hampering candidates' abilities to adopt new-style campaigns. According to the decision of the U.S. Court of Appeals for the Eighth Circuit, ACORN indicated that its intention was to "change the nature of local campaigns away from 'hot-button sound bites' in thirty-second television commercials to a substantive discussion of the issues."[28] The Court's decision, however, held that these limits violated contributors' rights of free speech and association without serving the compelling government interest of preventing bribery.[29] A similar case emerged after the state of Minnesota enacted a law limiting individual contributions to political committees to just $100 per election. After citing *Buckley*, the decision went on to note that such extreme limits were too low to allow contributors meaningful participation in the protected areas of speech and association.

The decision was appealed, but the Supreme Court refused to grant a writ of certiorari.[30] As a result, similar legal standards were applied in 1998 and 1999 to overturn comparably low contribution limits enacted by the state of Arkansas and the city of Akron, Ohio.[31]

THE SUPREME COURT DEVELOPS A MORE LENIENT STAN-
DARD   A more recent Supreme Court decision, stemming once again from Missouri, suggests a more lenient approach to contribution limits. Yet it still remains unclear how low will be considered too low by the courts. After the Missouri contribution limits enacted by public referendum were overruled, the state reverted to limits enacted by the legislature. These limits, which ranged from $1,075 down to $275, depending on the state office sought, were overturned by the same federal appellate court that had rejected the more stringent limits enacted by referendum.[32] The Supreme Court heard the case and reversed the decision, indicating that the limits in question were obviously a response to public perceptions of corruption and did not violate any rights of free speech or association. In doing so, it also encouraged a broader definition of corruption than simply preventing actual or perceived bribery.[33] According to the majority opinion,

> In speaking of "improper influence" and "opportunities for abuse" in addition to "quid pro quo arrangements" we recognized [in *Buckley*] a concern not confined to bribery of public officials, but extending to the broader threat from politicians too compliant with the wishes of large contributors.[34]

The new standard had an immediate effect on the types of laws upheld. Around the same time, federal trial and appellate courts both concluded that Maine's recently enacted $250 limit on contributions to state Senate and state House candidates did not violate the First Amendment and thus upheld them.[35] In addition, the low contribution levels once overturned in Akron were recently reestablished after being upheld at the appellate level.[36]

The Problem of Undue Influence Remains Unresolved

These cases serve as an indicator that achieving campaign finance reform in local governments will not be an easy task. The thorny problem of how to restrain the undue influence of monied interests has not been resolved at the national level, and local government reformers should expect to meet similar roadblocks. Quite simply, the Supreme Court's determination that both campaign spending and contributions are the equivalent of political speech worthy of at least some First Amendment protection means that many options are apt to be challenged and overturned in court. Clearly, though, innovation at the state and local levels has been responsible for pushing, and sometimes expanding, the limits on campaign finance reform outlined by the *Buckley* decision. Continued innovation will familiarize judges with concerns emerging at the local level and will, it is hoped, provide reformers in local, state, and national political arenas with more flexibility in their ability to respond to citizen concerns.

Supporting Disadvantaged Candidates

As with concern over large campaign contributions, dissatisfaction with the inherent advantages of incumbency and socioeconomic status is not new to observers of the U.S. political system. With the rise of new-style campaigns in national and state government races, incumbents' re-election rates sky-rocketed.[37] For example, re-election rates in the U.S. House of Representatives peaked at 98 percent in 1986 and 1988. Even in 1994, a year characterized by resentment of Washington, D.C., insiders, nine out of ten members were returned to office.[38] Yet competition is a prerequisite for the fulfillment of elections' democratic purpose. When no viable challenger is present in an election, voters have little choice but to return an incumbent to office even if his or her performance has been unsatisfactory. In addition, members of the upper class enjoy financial advantages similar to those of incumbents, which raises suspicions that the makeup of U.S. governing institutions is affected by average citizens' inability to mount comparable campaign efforts.

The Feasibility of Leveling the Playing Field

As these same concerns for competition and upper-class advantages inevitably emerge at the state and local level, efforts have been made to level the political playing field by restraining incumbents' and upper-class candidates' access to financial resources. Efforts to directly prohibit candidates from spending personal money on their own campaigns have no chance of withstanding a judicial challenge. For example, the campaign finance laws enacted by Congress in the 1970s restricted the amount of money that wealthy federal candidates could contribute to their own electoral efforts, but this provision was overturned by the Supreme Court as a violation of free speech rights.[39] More recently, a Kentucky law prohibiting gubernatorial candidates who refused public funding, and the accompanying expenditure limits, from making contributions to themselves in the twenty-eight days prior to a primary or general election was ruled unconstitutional.[40]

AN ATTEMPT TO ELIMINATE WAR CHESTS IN MISSOURI   The legal standard on more creative attempts to level the playing field is less clear.

Some such efforts at the state level have been overruled. The state of Missouri tried to equalize the financial resources available to incumbents and challengers. Missouri incumbents were briefly prevented from hoarding money donated to previous campaigns for use in future re-election efforts, as they were required to either turn over unspent contributions to the Missouri Ethics Commission or return them to contributors. Although officeholders would still be able to raise money more easily than their challengers, they would no longer possess intimidating war chests to scare away potential opponents. The well-intentioned law, however, was challenged and overturned because it effectively imposed expenditure limits on future campaigns, thus constituting an infringement of free speech.[41]

EFFORTS TO BALANCE CANDIDATE RESOURCES IN MINNESOTA AND MAINE   In Minnesota, one section of a campaign finance law was intended to level the playing field between publicly financed candidates and wealthy political actors who make independent expenditures. The law increased the spending limits imposed on those accepting public financing by the amount spent on independent expenditures against them. It also provided them with an additional public subsidy equal to half the amount of the independent expenditure. The law was overturned by the Eighth Circuit Court of Appeals because it encouraged self-censorship and chilled protected speech in the form of independent expenditures.[42] Yet a nearly identical law in the state of Maine has been upheld. The First Circuit Court of Appeals explicitly rejected the legal reasoning provided in deciding the prior case because it "equates responsive speech with an impairment to the initial speaker."[43]

Given these contradictory decisions, the Supreme Court may be looking for a test case in order to clarify its standards on legislative efforts to level the playing field among various types of political actors. Only time will tell whether legal challenges in response to state and local innovation will once again yield a decision that stretches limitations of *Buckley*. In the meantime, rather than waiting for a test case to be found, a more immediate way to diminish inequalities among candidates would be to enhance the resources available to challengers and average citizens interested in running for office.

Service Parties As a Remedy

Institutions ideally situated to provide this type of assistance to disadvantaged candidates are political parties because they are the sole type of organization with the primary goal of electing officials to public office. As such, they have a built-in incentive to improve their candidates' abilities to run for office. Out-of-office parties have a vested interest in recruiting and promoting challengers. Yet as success in local political arenas becomes associated with new-style strategies, the type of aid needed to run a competitive race also shifts. Although local candidates may still want help with traditional grassroots activities, they will also need increased financial assistance and the provision of professional campaign services.

Just as the problems encountered in the face of new-style local campaigns are not original, neither is the suggested solution. Any student of political parties will recognize this description of the current national and state "service parties." After highly successful fundraising efforts, the Republican National Committee began providing candidates with this type of assistance in the 1970s. The Democrats, as well as many of both parties' state committees, were quick to follow suit. At that point in time, the parties had suffered substantial blows to their role in the electoral process. They had lost exclusive control of nominating decisions and faced declining partisan identification in the electorate. Moreover, the increasing accessibility of communication technology enabled many candidates to carry their messages to the electorate largely without the assistance of party organizations. Initial accounts of these service-oriented activities were heralded as evidence that the political parties were evolving in order to play a role, albeit a less dominant one, in an electoral arena dominated by candidate-centered campaigns. As new-style local campaigns become commonplace, local party organizations may find it necessary to undergo a similar transformation. Not only would such changes help the parties to maintain a role in local electoral processes, they would enhance competition and representation by helping both challengers and less-advantaged candidates run competitive races.[44]

THE CONTROVERSY OVER SERVICE PARTIES   However, a recommendation to increase the candidate services supplied by local political party organizations may be controversial. Studies of party organizations have been criticized for focusing on service provision and for failing to assess the health of partisanship in the electorate. Some conclude that parties cannot accurately be described as resurgent until they once again fulfill the linkage function between the electorate and their representatives.[45] Another position, taking this argument an important step further, directly attributes the electorate's movement away from partisan attachments to the development of service parties because the parties have replaced direct contact with communication technology and now focus on serving candidates.[46] According to this perspective, "instead of considering voters the primary client of the party, cultivating their loyalties and activating them on election day, service-oriented parties strive to please candidates."[47] The results are baseless parties supported by the elite who benefit from their services, but not by average citizens. Thus the concern is that because of service parties, "the nature of the democratic process may be shifting to the elite pole."[48]

Concerns over appropriate party functions in a democratic system are legitimate. Yet given the current context of local elections, service parties may actually help avoid such fears by preventing an elite-dominated political process. Surely, such a support system would enhance the recruitment of average citizens. If, for example, the Albany County Republican Party had been prepared to provide campaign services in the 1970s, someone other than a millionaire entrepreneur might have been willing to challenge Erastus Corning. Without such assistance, many average citizens will assume, probably correctly, that they do not have the capacity to mount a competitive campaign.

THE WIDESPREAD RELIANCE ON NONPARTISAN ELECTIONS
Such arguments in favor of local service parties are, however, largely moot because approximately three-quarters of the municipalities in the United States have adopted nonpartisan elections.[49] Nonpartisanship was a reform promoted by the Progressive Movement and Municipal Reform Movement as a way to eliminate the corruption of machines, to remove state and national issues from local politics, to emphasize candidates' individual qualifications over partisan affiliations, and to elect a different type of municipal officer. While nonpartisanship accomplished these intentions, research over the years indicates that the lack of a party infrastructure to organize opposition and recruit candidates also leads to fewer successful challengers and to more candidates with advantaged backgrounds.[50] Unfortunately, unless municipalities revert en masse to partisan elections or develop alternative support systems for disadvantaged candidates, this pattern will only be exacerbated by the trend toward new-style local campaigns.

Conclusion
This review of available remedies admittedly offers no single, simple solution to return America's elections to their intended function. Those frustrated by the effects of sophisticated electoral efforts can no longer be comforted by the preservation of traditional grassroots campaigns in smaller communities. New-style campaigns, and the troubling concerns accompanying them, are a growing presence in local political arenas. At last, the heightened concerns over undue influence and disadvantaged candidates have infiltrated all planes of the U.S. federal system. Reforms available to correct these detrimental effects are not readily apparent. The most obvious solutions to the problem of undue influence, such as campaign expenditure limits and restraints on incumbents' and upper-class candidates' spending advantages, have been blocked by court decisions that equate campaign spending with political speech. Meanwhile, disadvantaged candidates could be supported by local service parties. Yet the development of such organizations is hindered by the U.S. municipalities' widespread reliance on nonpartisan elections. The lack of a quick fix is made even more troubling by the fact that these negative

consequences are compounded in smaller political units. Hence, while the use of communication technology holds out the enticing potential of improving information environments in local government races, any benefits to be gained have been overshadowed by these troubling consequences.

At the same time, the persistent innovation taking place in America's state and local governing institutions provides reason to hope that electoral processes will be reformed. Challenges to state and local campaign finance laws in court have already yielded some success in stretching the legal standards imposed by *Buckley*. Although reform cannot be achieved in one broad stroke, creative responses to public demands for accountability in the electoral process will continue. And these responses will chip away at the problems plaguing American elections. The number of people involved in the U.S. political system increases exponentially when state and local government officers are included in the summary. The creative energy they can contribute to the resolution of public problems should not be underestimated. They are the reason why multiple policy-making centers have long been recognized as federalism's strength. Optimists note that the grass roots has been the staging ground for every other major political reform effort in the United States.[51] Once such efforts take hold across America's cities and towns, in our neighborhoods and communities, they are nearly impossible to stop. Perhaps, then, we can take the local activity described here as a sign that "the drive for campaign finance reform, and for even broader democratic political reform, is on the cusp of becoming another major movement."[52]

While focusing attention on the specific problems facing local government electoral districts, this research serves as a reminder that the contexts of U.S. political processes are dynamic. As circumstances change, so, too, must the democratic institutions that once performed satisfactorily. One should cherish the function of accountability that elections were intended to provide, rather than the structure of elections created by current electoral regulations. Fortunately, this sentiment is ingrained in the American political culture. As a result, Americans have been willing, and often quite eager, to promote reforms intended to improve their political processes. One can hope that attention from multiple policy-making centers, combined with America's reformist sentiment, will eventually prove successful in diminishing the harmful side effects of new-style campaigns.

Notes

1. Jonathan M. Rich, "Campaign Finance Legislation: Equality and Freedom," *Columbia Journal of Law and Social Problems* 20 (1986): 411.

2. "The Inauguration: We Force the Spring," *New York Times*, 21 January 1993, 15(A).

3. Dan Lynch, "Examining the Price of Elected Office," *Times Union* (Albany, N.Y.), 4 September 1997, 1(D).

4. Lynch, "Examining the Price," 1(D).

5. *Buckley v. Valeo*, 46 L. Ed. 2d 659, 688 (1976).

6. *Buckley v. Valeo*, 704 (1976).

7. *Buckley v. Valeo*, 704 (1976).

8. For example, in *First National Bank of Boston v. Belloti*, 435 U.S. 765 (1978), the Court invalidated a prohibition on corporate contributions and expenditures in ballot issues because the risk of bribing a public official was not a concern. Again in *Citizens against Rent Control v. Berkley*, 454 U.S. 290 (1981), the Court overturned an ordinance limiting contributions to ballot issues because it failed to further the prevention of quid pro quo corruption. A final example is *Federal Election Commission v. National Conservative PAC*, 470 U.S. 480 (1985), when the Court overturned limits on independent spending by political action committees on behalf of publicly financed candidates, based on the reasoning that the limits were not justified by preventing bribery.

9. *Local Campaign Finance Reform: Case Studies in Innovation and Model Legislation* (Denver, Colo.: National Civic League, 1998). According to the Crested Butte city attorney, the ordinance was still in place as of October 2001.

10. *Kruse v. City of Cincinnati*, 142 F.3d 907 (1998).

11. As quoted by Robert Zausner, "Campaign Spending Limit?" *Philadelphia Inquirer*, 23 October 1998, 21(A).

12. As quoted by Zausner, "Campaign Spending Limit?" 21(A).

13. As quoted by Zausner, "Campaign Spending Limit?" 21(A).

14. Zausner, "Campaign Spending Limit?" 21(A).

15. Zausner, "Campaign Spending Limit?" 21(A).

16. Zausner, "Campaign Spending Limit?" 21(A).

17. Zausner, "Campaign Spending Limit?" 21(A); and Margie Baca Archuleta, Albuquerque city clerk, correspondence with J. Cherie Strachan, September 2001.

18. For a thorough discussion of state programs, see Michael J. Malbin and Thomas L. Gais, *The Day after Reform, Sobering Campaign Finance Lessons from the American States* (Albany, N.Y.: Rockefeller Institute Press, 1998), 22–24 and 51.

19. *Local Campaign Finance Reform: Case Studies in Innovation and Model Legislation*.

20. *Addendum to Local Campaign Finance Reform: Case Studies in Innovation and Model Legislation* (Denver, Colo: National Civic League, 2001), 18–19.

21. Joyce Brown, Chapel Hill councilwoman, telephone interview by J. Cherie Strachan. Tape recording, October 2001.

22. *Local Campaign Finance Reform: Case Studies in Innovation and Model Legislation*.

23. *Shrink Missouri Government PAC v. Maupin*, 71 F.3d.1422, 1424 (1995).

24. *Local Campaign Finance Reform: Case Studies in Innovation and Model Legislation;* and Rita Harris, Fort Collins deputy clerk, telephone interview by J. Cherie Strachan. Tape recording, October 2001.

25. *Local Campaign Finance Reform: Case Studies in Innovation and Model Legislation.*

26. *Buckley v. Valeo,* 689 (1976).

27. For a detailed account of the law, see *Carver v. Nixon,* 72 F.3d 633 (1995).

28. *Carver v. Nixon,* 633 (1995).

29. *Carver v. Nixon,* 643 (1995).

30. *Day v. Holahan,* 34 F.3d 1356, 1365 (1994).

31. *Russell v. Burris,* 146 F.3d 563 (1998); and *Frank v. City of Akron,* 95 F.2d. 706 (1999).

32. *Shrink Missouri Government PAC v. Adams,* 161 F.3d 519 (1998).

33. *Nixon v. Shrink Missouri Government PAC,* 120 S.Ct. 897 (2000).

34. *Nixon v. Shrink Missouri Government,* 941.

35. *Daggett v. Webster,* 81 F.2d 128 (2000); and *Daggett v. Commissioner on Governmental Ethics and Election Practices,* 205 F.3d 445 (2000).

36. *Frank v. City of Akron,* 2002 US App Lexis 9598; 2002 Fed App 081P (6th Cir).

37. Jonathan S. Krasno, *Challengers, Competition, and Reelection* (New Haven, Conn.: Yale University Press, 1994).

38. Daniel M. Shea and Stephen C. Brooks, "How to Topple an Incumbent," *Campaigns & Elections* 16 (June 1995): 20–29.

39. *Buckley v. Valeo,* 704 (1976).

40. *Gable v. Patton,* 142 F.3d 940 (1998).

41. *Shrink Missouri Government PAC v. Maupin,* 1427 (1995).

42. *Day v. Holahan,* 1360 (1994).

43. *Daggett v. Commission on Governmental Ethics and Election Practices,* 445 (2000).

44. This suggestion that service parties may be beneficial corresponds to Kolodny's claim that consultants can help parties bridge the communication gap between party in government and party in the electorate in an era of advanced communication technology. Robin Kolodny, "Political Consultants and Political Parties," in *Campaign Warriors: The Role of Political Consultants in Elections,* ed. James A. Thurber and Candice J. Nelson (Washington, D.C.: Brookings Institution Press, 2000), 130.

45. John J. Coleman, "Resurgent or Just Busy? Party Organizations in Contemporary America," in *The State of the Parties,* ed. John C. Green and Daniel M. Shea (Lanham, Md.: Rowman & Littlefield, 1996), 367–84.

46. Daniel M. Shea, "The Passing of Realignment and the Advent of the 'Base-Less' Party System," *American Politics Quarterly* 27, no. 1 (January 1999): 33–57.

47. Shea, "The Passing of Realignment," 45.

48. Shea, "The Passing of Realignment," 53.

49. Victor S. DeSantis and Tari Renner, "Contemporary Patterns and Trends in Municipal Government Structure," *The Municipal Yearbook: 1993* (Washington, D.C.: International City/County Management Association, 1993).

50. See Carol A. Cassel, "Social Background Characteristics of Nonpartisan City Council Members," *Western Political Quarterly* 38 (September 1985): 495–501; John J. Kirlen, "Electoral Conflict and Democracy in Cities," *Journal of Politics* 37 (February 1975): 262–69; and Brian F. Schaffner, Matthew J. Streb, and Gerald C. Wright, "A Rule That Works: The Nonpartisan Ballot in State and Local Elections" (paper presented at the Midwest Political Science Association Meeting, Chicago, April 1999).

51. Ric Bainter and Paul Lhevine, "Political Reform Comes from Communities," *National Civic Review* 87, no. 1 (Spring 1998): 58.

52. Bainter and Lhevine, "Political Reform Comes from Communities," 58.

APPENDIX A: A DETAILED ACCOUNT OF DATA COLLECTION

The Mail Survey of General Political Consultants

The decision to post questionnaires to consultants rather than to candidates was driven by the sheer number of elected officers in the United States. Local governments, including counties, municipalities, and special districts, are scattered across the country. Examining the campaigns of all or even a sample of the candidates who ran for public offices in this vast array of local governments would be a prohibitive task. A simpler way to gauge whether these candidates have turned to sophisticated campaign tactics is to determine whether they have hired professionals to provide expert assistance in using those tactics. Some local government candidates may adopt sophisticated tactics by seeking out pro bono assistance or by attempting to master the necessary communication technology. The expertise needed to accomplish tasks such as conducting a public opinion poll or producing a television commercial, however, requires most candidates to rely on professionals.

A questionnaire was designed to explore whether consultants are working with different types of local government candidates, the types of tactics and professional services their local clients are using, and the role that consultants play in their campaigns. Two sources exist for identifying political consultants. The profession's primary trade journal, *Campaigns & Elections*, publishes an annual political services issue listing political consultants who provide various kinds of campaign services. The March 1998 issue was used. The American Association of Political Consultants also publishes an annual *Political Resources Directory*, and the 1997 directory was used.[1] Both sources categorize consultants by their specialties. As the profession of political consulting has evolved, more consultants began specializing in providing a particular service, such as media production, public opinion polling, volunteer

123

training, or demographic voter targeting.² Some, however, still work as general consultants who provide a broader array of services and strategic advice to their clients. Candidates may hire a general consultant, as well as several other specialists, throughout the course of a campaign. Yet since generalists play a more sustained role in their clients' campaigns, they are familiar with the entire campaign process, rather than with only one particular aspect of the campaign. Even if they are not providing a particular professional service, general consultants should know whether it was provided by another consultant. As a result, the decision was made to include only general consultants in the survey. Questionnaires were mailed to general consulting firms listed in either one or both of these sources.

While the combination of these two sources provides the most complete listing of consultants available, it cannot provide a comprehensive account of every consultant working in the United States. People who earn money working on campaigns are not compelled to join a professional association or to advertise in their profession's trade magazine. Yet many of these types of consultants may be listed in these two sources. Less well-known consultants would benefit more from advertising in a magazine that reaches a national audience than would their visible counterparts in the profession. In addition, local consultants who aspire to work in national and statewide contexts may join the American Association of Political Consultants in order to network with other consultants. Although the list of consultants generated from these two sources will inevitably exclude some in the profession, it will still provide an indicator of whether consultants are working with local government candidates.

At the same time, several factors indicate that the consultants with local clientele who received the questionnaire were more likely to return it than were others. First, mail surveys provide limited interaction between subjects and researchers. Although incentives encouraging participation can be provided, persuasion is limited by the lack of direct contact. As a result, those who respond do so at their own initiative, and they may choose to respond because they have a predisposed interest in the research topic. Second, the general consultants who received the questionnaire were offered the survey results as an incentive to participate.³ Consultants working with local candidates would find this information useful for evaluating their competition, whereas those working exclusively with national and state candidates would find it less relevant. Finally, some prominent consultants tend to be disdainful of work with local government candidates. One consultant, well known in the consulting profession for his work on statewide races, returned the survey along with the following comment:

> No one would contract a small race except through economic necessity. That usually means that the firm has too little recognition

to compete in the large arena. Small races are as much work as a large campaign, and one must deal with unsophisticated candidates and workers. It is really a chore that I am glad to say is in my distant past.

Prominent consultants sharing this attitude may have failed to return the questionnaire not only because they think the topic is uninteresting or irrelevant to them, but because they think it is unimportant. Thus, the survey results cannot be used to make generalizable claims about the entire population of political consultants. The results will, however, provide insight into the subset of political consultants that serves candidates running in smaller electoral districts.

A mailing list for the general consultants listed in *Campaigns & Elections'* March 1998 issue was easy to compile. Each of the entries under general consultants included the name of an individual consultant and a complete address. The organization of the *1997 Political Services Directory* made compiling a mailing list more difficult. The directory lists the names and telephone numbers of general consulting firms in one index, but the owners of the firms were listed in a separate index. Neither index included a mailing address. The names of individual consultants associated with each firm were identified by cross-referencing the two indices. If more than one principal was listed for a particular firm, the consultant whose name was incorporated into the firm's title was used as the recipient of the questionnaire. In other cases, the recipient was selected at random from the list of principals. Next, the addresses of as many firms as possible were located through telephone directories. When a firm was not listed in the Yellow Pages, telephone calls were made to ask for an address.

After eliminating firms for a variety of reasons, including duplicate listings in both directories, location in a foreign country, or going out of business, a list of 607 valid addresses was compiled. After two waves of mailings, 185 of the 607 valid questionnaires were returned, producing a response rate of a slightly more than 30 percent.

The Telephone Interviews with Local Political Reporters

The decision to conduct telephone interviews with political reporters in midsized cities with a mayor-council form of government was also driven by the vast number of local government units in the United States. The decision to focus on midsized cities, with populations ranging from 50,000 to 250,000 residents, was made because journalists' accounts indicate that candidates in America's largest cities began running sophisticated campaigns as early as the

1970s.[4] The explanation for their innovation is obvious. With large electoral districts, these candidates could benefit from the broadcast technology available at the time, and they could raise the money to purchase it from a larger pool of potential supporters. Identifying whether these tactics have spread to midsized cities represents the next step. Excluding other local government entities such as towns and townships with midsized populations, as well as cities with fewer than 50,000 residents, helps limit the local electoral districts included in the research to a manageable number. It will also help to determine whether the effort it would take to explore the sizable number of smaller local political units in the United States is warranted.

The decision to study mayoral candidates was made because knowledge about mayoral campaigns improves understanding of the broader universe of local government races. The mayorship is often perceived as the primary position of political leadership for a municipality. As a single office, the position is more visible to the public than are executive commissions or legislative bodies. A mayor is also perceived by the public as having more responsibilities and greater political powers than other elected officers have in the local government. As such, the mayorship is a prestigious position that should attract politically ambitious candidates who are more likely to adopt new campaign tactics. In addition, mayors typically serve a larger constituency, allowing them to benefit more from sophisticated tactics and to raise the money to purchase these from a larger pool of supporters. As a result, one can speculate about the activities of other local government candidates based on the types of campaigns conducted by mayoral candidates. If candidates in a competitive mayoral race have not adopted sophisticated tactics, it is improbable that other municipal candidates in the same city will use them. Finally, focusing on mayoral, rather than legislative, candidates also made the research more manageable. The number of campaigns to study was limited because there are simply far fewer mayoral candidates. In addition, the focus on a single, prominent race in each city facilitated interviews with reporters.

To develop a list of the cities meeting these two criteria, cities with midsized populations were identified using U.S. Census of Populations estimates for 1994.[5] Those cities with populations ranging between 50,000 and 250,000 residents were then cross-referenced with the International City/County Management Association's *1996 Municipal Yearbook*, which lists the forms of government used by U.S. municipalities.[6] A total of 142 cities had both an appropriate population size and a mayor-council form of government.[7] It should be noted that this research design focuses on the cities meeting these two criteria, rather than on equal representation of states or regions of the country. In fact, 12 states have no cities meeting these criteria.[8] Nor are the 142 cities equally distributed across the remaining 38 states.

The interviews were conducted with the local political reporters who had covered the most recent mayoral election in these cities. Local newspapers were identified in the *Editor & Publisher Yearbook*, which lists all daily papers published in the United States in alphabetical order by state.[9] A few of the 142 cities do not have daily papers. In these cases, the staffs in the mayors' offices were called and asked to identify the newspaper providing the most coverage of local politics. Sometimes the appropriate newspaper was a weekly, rather than a daily, paper. In other cases, suburban cities were covered by daily newspapers in a nearby city. A researcher identified reporters by calling newsrooms and asking to speak to the local political reporter.

Although the mayoral candidates were more familiar with their own campaigns, this design relies on reporters as the source of information for a number of reasons. First, reporters' training, both in college courses and on the job, socializes them to adhere to the norm of objectivity. Thus, they are more likely to provide an unbiased account of candidates' activities and have less incentive to misrepresent information about the campaigns. Second, unlike politicians, who tend to be suspicious of questions about their campaigns, reporters regularly disseminate information about campaign practices to the public. In fact, most of the reporters contacted seemed sympathetic to a researcher seeking an interview—probably because interviews are the primary way that they gather information for news stories. As long as they were not writing under a deadline, most were willing, and some quite eager, to be interviewed. Finally, reporters should be familiar with the types of information requested. The questions about mayoral campaigns asked for basic, descriptive information such as the type of tactic used and the amount of money spent. Each reporter was also asked for information about the city's political environment, government structure, other local candidates, and previous mayoral candidates, which they were more likely to know than current candidates.

Reporters should also be familiar with this basic information about campaigns because they indicated that such subjects were important topics of coverage to their newspapers. Reporters were asked to rate both the importance of covering local politics in general and of covering local elections to their newspapers. When rating the importance of local political coverage on a scale of 1 to 10, most reporters responded with a 10. Seventy percent gave the topic high importance by selecting an 8, a 9, or a 10. Meanwhile, only 6 percent rated the topic of local politics with less than a 5. Even more reporters indicated that covering local elections was important to their papers. Only 2 percent rated it with less than a 6. Once again, most reporters responded with a 10, and 85 percent gave the topic high importance by choosing the ratings of an 8, a 9, or a 10. Since the respondents were responsible for providing coverage of these important topics, they should be familiar with basic information about them.

The quality of information provided by reporters was enhanced by their predilection for factual accuracy. When asked, for example, to estimate candidates' spending, they were reluctant to answer unless they knew the exact amount. Many insisted on checking old stories, rather than relying on their memories. Reporters were ready to admit when they did not know the answers to questions and were willing to recommend other sources for the desired information. In cases where reporters did not know information, follow-up telephone calls were made to candidates or their staffs, board of election or city clerks, and/or other experts.

As a result, telephone interviews were completed in 109 of the 142 cities, producing a response rate of nearly 77 percent. Altogether, information was collected about the campaigns of 217 candidates who ran in these 109 cities' most recent mayoral elections. Some of these candidates were unopposed, whereas others ran in two-candidate and multiple-candidate races. In multiple-candidate races, reporters were asked to exclude information about fringe candidates who had made little or no campaigning efforts.

Notes

1. Carol Hess, ed., *Political Resource Directory 1997* (Burlington, Vt.: Political Resources Inc., 1997).

2. Robert V. Friedenberg, *Political Consultants in Political Campaigns* (Westport, Conn.: Praeger, 1997).

3. In order to provide results while guaranteeing respondents' anonymity, consultants were provided with a postcard, which could be mailed separately from their responses, to request the survey findings.

4. Jerry Hagstrom and Robert Guskind, "Mayoral Candidates Enter the Big Time Using Costly TV Ads and Consultants," *National Journal* (6 April 1985): 737.

5. Population estimates were obtained from the U.S. Bureau of the Census, *County and City Databook: 1994* (Washington, D.C.: U.S. Government Printing Office, 1994).

6. *The Municipal Yearbook, 1996* (Washington D.C.: International City/County Management Association, 1996).

7. Albany, New York, which meets both criteria, was excluded from the database as the city was used for exploratory research. In addition, the questions for the telephone interviews with local reporters were pretested with the local political reporter at the city's newspaper, the *Times Union*.

8. These states are Arizona, Colorado, Georgia, Hawaii, Maine, Maryland, Missouri, Montana, Nevada, New Mexico, Oklahoma, and Vermont.

9. *1997 Editor & Publisher Yearbook* (New York: Editor & Publisher Company, 1997).

APPENDIX B: SUMMARIZING CAMPAIGN SOPHISTICATION

The measure of campaign sophistication used for this analysis relies on a simple index that equally weights the use of four sophisticated tactics—public opinion polls, television ads, targeted direct mail, and radio ads. Yet some of these tactics rely on communication technology that is both more complex and difficult to master. The complexity of a particular tactic is signified by the relationship between its use and hiring a corresponding specialist, which explains why candidates are more apt to hire help with a public opinion poll than with a radio ad. Hence, another aspect of campaign sophistication, in addition to the total number of tactics used, is the complexity of the tactics used.

The fact that certain tactics are more difficult to incorporate suggests that the data would be naturally weighted. Candidates who are capable of incorporating the more complex tactics should also be able to use simpler ones. For example, candidates using the most complex tactic of public opinion polling should also have the knowledge and/or resources needed to use the remaining three sophisticated tactics. Similarly, candidates using television advertisements should also be able to use the two easier tactics. Finally, those using direct mail should also have the capacity to air radio advertisements. To determine whether candidates could be rank ordered in this fashion to efficiently incorporate tactic complexity into the measure of campaign sophistication, a Guttman scale was constructed.

Table B.1 reveals that this pattern of use did occur, as 61 percent of the mayoral candidates' campaign activities form a scalar structure. These candidates were assigned Guttman scale scores, permitting the most accurate reproduction of their campaign activities. A scale score of four indicates that each sophisticated tactic was used, while a three means all but the most difficult tactic was used. Meanwhile, a score of two shows that the candidate relied on both direct mail and radio, while a one indicates that only the easiest tactic of radio was used. Although 61 percent accuracy is impressive, 39 percent of the candidates fail to conform to a scalar structure.

Perhaps a perfect Guttman scale is not achievable because factors other than complexity affect candidates' use of particular tactics. A plausible explanation is that candidates need to consider both budgetary constraints and electoral district characteristics. Money is rarely an unlimited resource in a campaign. Those seeking public office must decide which tactics are most beneficial to their efforts. For example, a candidate who wants to spend his or her funds on a professional pollster may decide to rely on direct mail and/or radio in lieu of an expensive television advertisement. In other circumstances, a particular tactic may be easier to use, but less helpful in a given electoral district. If local radio station audiences do not overlap with appropriate voter groups, a candidate will turn to other tactics, even though radio advertisements are less complex. Hence, a candidate running a very sophisticated campaign may rely on all other sophisticated tactics without turning to radio.

Accommodations can be made to include candidates such as these, whose use of sophisticated tactics varied from the scalar structure, in the Guttman

Table B.1   Use of Sophisticated Tactics Produces a Natural Scale

	P	T	DM	R	Prediction Error	# of Cases	Total Error
Scale Types							
	1	1	1	1	0	42	0
	0	1	1	1	0	26	0
	0	0	1	1	0	28	0
	0	0	0	1	0	8	0
	0	0	0	0	0	27	0
						131	0
Mixed Types							
	1	1	1	0	1	11	11
	1	1	0	1	1	4	4
	1	0	1	1	1	8	8
	1	1	0	0	2	2	4
	1	0	1	0	2	10	20
	1	0	0	1	2	4	8
	1	0	0	0	1	2	2
	0	1	1	0	1	8	8
	0	1	0	1	1	5	5
	0	1	0	0	1	0	0
	0	0	1	0	1	29	29
						83	99

N = 214. 0 indicates a tactic was not used; 1 indicates a tactic was used. The abbreviated column headings represent the key sophisticated tactics counted. P = Public Opinion Polls; T = Television Ads; DM = Targeted Direct Mail; and R = Radio Ads.
Source: 1998 interviews about the most recent mayoral candidates in midsized cities.

scale. To do so, they were assigned scale scores reducing the number of errors made when predicting the campaign tactics used. For example, a candidate using only public opinion polls was assigned a scale score of zero. The score results in only one error because it accurately summarizes the candidate's use of the three easiest tactics, while inaccurately predicting the use of one tactic—the public opinion poll. Similarly, a candidate using all of the tactics except radio advertisements was assigned a score of four. The score conveys accurate information about the use of all tactics except radio advertisements. These scoring accommodations were required in order to include all the cases in the Guttman scale. Table B.1 indicates, however, that most could be assigned a score producing only one prediction error. As a result, the coefficient of reproducibility, or the percentage of tactics accurately predicted by the scale, is 88 percent.[1] Although this coefficient is less than ideal, it is close to the commonly used standard of 90 percent.[2]

The process of creating the Guttman scale revealed that most candidates using more complex tactics also relied on all the simpler ones. Sixty-one percent could be classified as scale types. Yet plotting the tactics used by candidates classified as mixed types also supports this revelation. Of all the candidates who used a public opinion poll, only two failed to use additional sophisticated tactics. Meanwhile, all of the candidates whose most complex tactic was a television advertisement relied on direct mail and/or radio advertisements. The only discrepancy in this pattern is the comparatively large number of candidates whose sole sophisticated tactic was the use of direct mail. This pattern probably occurred because direct mail, which can be used to carefully target small groups of voters, is particularly useful in local races. The natural order of the data automatically produces higher index scores for candidates relying on more complex tactics. As a result, the decision was made to use the simple, summary measure, rather than the Guttman scale or a weighted index.

Notes

1. This percentage is calculated by dividing accurate predictions by the total number of responses.

2. Earl Babbie, *Survey Research Methods,* 2d ed. (Belmont, Calif.: Wadsworth, 1990), 170.

REFERENCES

Argetsinger, Amy. "Crowded Field Running for Annapolis Mayor." *Washington Post,* 14 September 1997, 5(B).

Addendum to Local Campaign Finance Reform: Case Studies in Innovation and Model Legislation. Denver, Colo.: National Civic League, 2001.

Agranoff, Robert. *The New Style in Election Campaigns.* Boston: Holbrook, 1972.

Baca Archuleta, Margie, Albuquerque city clerk. Correspondence with J. Cherie Strachan, September 2001.

Babbie, Earl. *Survey Research Methods,* 2d ed. Belmont, Calif.: Wadsworth, 1990.

Bainter, Ric, and Paul Lhevine, "Political Reform Comes from Communities." *National Civic Review* 87, no. 1 (Spring 1998): 57–65.

Beaudry, Ann, and Bob Schaeffer. *Winning Local and State Elections: The Guide to Organizing Your Campaign.* New York: Free Press, 1986.

Bennett, D. L. "An Election Report, Lathem Funding Sets County Record." *Atlanta Journal Constitution,* 16 July 1998, 4(JQ).

Benson, Clea, and John Borland. "Professional Campaign Help Goes Local." *California Journal* (November 1994): 13–17.

Bibby, John F. "State Party Organizations: Coping and Adapting to Candidate Centered Politics." Pp. 23–49, in *The Parties Respond,* edited by Sandy L. Maisel. Boulder, Colo.: Westview, 1998.

Bishop, Bill. "Truth in Advertising." *Herald Leader* (Lexington, Ky.), 6 May 1998, 15(A).

Brown, Joyce, Chapel Hill councilwoman. Telephone interview by J. Cherie Strachan. Tape recording, October 2001.

Browning, Graeme. "Medium Cool." *National Journal* (19 October 1996): 2223.

Buckley v. Valeo, 46 L. Ed. 2d 659, 688 (1976).

Callahan, Dennis, Annapolis mayoral candidate. Interview by J. Cherie Strachan. Tape recording, September 2001.

Carver v. Nixon, 72 F.3d 633 (1995).

Cassel, Carol A. "Social Background Characteristics of Nonpartisan City Council Members." *Western Political Quarterly* 38 (September 1985): 495–501.

Citizens against Rent Control v. Berkley, 454 U.S. 290 (1981).

Cole, Christopher. "Bradenton, Fla., Campaign Aids Open Political Consulting Firm." *The Bradenton Herald,* 19 January 200, 2(A).

Coleman, John J. "Resurgent or Just Busy? Party Organizations in Contemporary America." Pp. 376–84, in *The State of the Parties,* edited by John C. Green and Daniel M. Shea. Lanham, Md.: Rowman & Littlefield, 1996.

Cotter, Cornelius P., James L. Gibson, John F. Bibby, and Robert Huckshorn. *Party Organization in American Politics.* New York: Praeger, 1984.

Daggett v. Commissioner on Governmental Ethics and Election Practices, 205 F.3d 445 (2000).

Daggett v. Webster, 81 F.2d 128 (2000).

Darcy, R., Susan Welch, and Janet Clark. *Women, Elections and Representation.* Lincoln: University of Nebraska Press, 1994.

Day v. Holahan, 34 F.3d 1356, 1365 (1994).

Dayton Daily News, 3 October–13 December 1997.

DeSantis, Victor S., and Tari Renner. "Contemporary Patterns and Trends in Municipal Government Structure." *The Municipal Yearbook: 1993.* Washington, D.C.: International City/County Management Association, 1993.

DeVries, Walter. "American Campaign Consulting: Trends and Concerns." *PS: Political Science* 22, no. 1 (March 1989): 21–25.

Dunn, Anita. "The Best Campaign Wins: Local Press Coverage of Nonpresidential Races." Pp. 112–25, in *Campaigns and Elections American Style,* edited by James A. Thurber and Candice J. Nelson. Boulder, Colo.: Westview, 1995.

Dye, Thomas. *Politics in States and Communities,* 7th ed. Englewood Cliffs, N.J.: Prentice Hall, 1991.

Elazar, Daniel. *Exploring Federalism.* Tuscaloosa: University of Alabama Press, 1987.

———. *American Federalism: A View from the States,* 2d ed. New York: Thomas Y. Crowell, 1972.

"Expense of Local Political Races Is Outrageous." *Las Vegas Review Journal,* 9 September 2000, 14(B).

Federal Election Commission v. National Conservative PAC, 470 U.S. 480 (1985).

"Fiercely Fought Campaign Nears End." *Bradenton Herald,* 24 October 1999, 1(B).

First National Bank of Boston v. Belloti, 435 U.S. 765 (1978).

Frank v. City of Akron, 95 F.2d. 706 (1999).

Friedenberg, Robert V. *Communication Consultants in Political Campaigns.* Westport, Conn.: Praeger, 1997.

Gable v. Patton, 142 F.3d 940 (1998).

Ginsberg, Benjamin. "A Post-Electoral Era?" *PS: Political Science* 22, no. 1 (March 1989): 18–20.

———. *The Captive Public.* New York: Basic, 1986.

Goodman, Vicky, Robey campaign adviser. Telephone interview by J. Cherie Strachan. Tape recording, October 2001.

Graber, Doris. *Processing the News: How People Tame the Information Tide*, 2d ed. New York: Longman, 1988.

Griswald, Lewis. "Visalia Council Race Shaping Up." *Fresno Bee*, 4 July 1997, 1.

Grondahl, Paul. *Mayor Corning: Albany Icon, Albany Enigma*. Albany, N.Y.: Washington Park Press, 1997.

Guskind, Robert. "Cable Connection." *National Journal* (19 September 1992): 2111.

Hagstrom, Jerry. "Spreading the Load." *National Journal* (19 September 1992): 2529–31.

Hagstrom, Jerry, and Robert Guskind. "Mayoral Candidates Enter the Big Time Using Costly TV Ads and Consultants." *National Journal* (6 April 1985): 737.

Harris, Rita, Fort Collins deputy clerk. Telephone interview by J. Cherie Strachan. Tape recording, October 2001.

Herrnson, Paul S. "Hired Guns and House Races: Campaign Professionals in House Elections." Pp. 65–90, in *Campaign Warriors: The Role of Political Consultants in Elections*, edited by James A. Nelson and Candice J. Nelson. Washington, D.C.: Brookings Institution Press, 2000.

———. "Field Work, Political Parties, and Volunteerism." Pp. 152–60, in *Campaigns and Elections American Style*, edited by James A. Thurber and Candice J. Nelson. Boulder, Colo.: Westview, 1995.

———. "National Party Organizations at the Century's End." Pp. 50–82, in *The Parties Respond*, edited by Sandy L. Maisel. Boulder, Colo.: Westview, 1988.

Hess, Carol, ed. *Political Resource Directory 1997*. Burlington, Vt.: Political Resources Inc., 1997.

Hoefler, James. "Cable Television Advertising and Subnational Elections." *Comparative State Politics* (April 1990): 37–42.

Jamieson, James B. "Some Social and Political Correlates of Incumbency in Municipal Elections." *Social Science Quarterly* 51, no. 4 (March 1971): 946–52.

Johnson, Dennis, Annapolis mayoral candidate. Telephone interview by J. Cherie Strachan. Tape recording, September 2001.

Johnson, Dennis. *No Place for Amateurs*. New York: Routledge, 2001.

———. "The Business of Political Consulting." Pp. 37–52, in *Campaign Warriors: The Role of Political Consultants in Elections*, edited by James A. Nelson and Candice J. Nelson. Washington D.C.: Brookings Institution Press, 2000.

Johnson, Nancy. "Running for Office Can Be an Education." *South Bend Tribune*, 30 April 2000, 1(F).

Johnson, Noel "Bud," Touhey campaign adviser. Interview by J. Cherie Strachan. Tape recording, Troy, N.Y., May 1998.

Just, Marion R., et al. *Crosstalk: Citizens, Candidates and the Media in a Presidential Election*. Chicago: University of Chicago Press, 1996.

Kaid, Lynda Lee. "Ethical Dimensions of Political Advertising." Pp. 145–65, in *Ethical Dimensions of Political Communication*, edited by Robert Denton. New York: Praeger, 1991.

Kendall, Veronica. Telephone interview by J. Cherie Strachan. Tape recording, September 2001.

Kirlen, John J. "Electoral Conflict and Democracy in Cities." *Journal of Politics* 37 (February 1975): 262–69.

Kolodny, Robin. "Political Consultants and Political Parties." Pp. 110–132, in *Campaign Warriors: The Role of Political Consultants in Elections*, edited by James A. Nelson and Candice J. Nelson. Washington D.C.: Brookings Institution Press, 2000.

Krasno, Jonathan S. *Challengers, Competition, and Reelection*. New Haven, Conn.: Yale University Press, 1994.

Kruse v. City of Cincinnati, 142 F.3d 907 (1998).

Landers, Don, Visalia mayor. Telephone interview by J. Cherie Strachan. Tape recording, October 2001.

Lawson, Debbie, Madison school board candidate. Telephone interview by J. Cherie Strachan. Tape recording, October 2001.

Lee, Mike. *Fort Worth Star Telegram* reporter. Telephone interview by J. Cherie Strachan. Tape recording, September 2001.

———. "Candidate Reflects on Loss in Race for Mayor." *Fort-Worth Star Telegram*, 12 May 2000, 1.

Lemke, Emily, Cherokee County chair. Telephone interview by J. Cherie Strachan. Tape recording, September 2001.

Luntz, Frank. *Candidates, Consultants and Campaigns*. New York: Basic, 1988.

Local Campaign Finance Reform: Case Studies in Innovation and Model Legislation. Denver, Colo.: National Civic League, 1998.

Madison, James. "Federalist #10." Pp. 77–84, in *The Federalist Papers*. New York: Penguin, 1961.

Maisel, Sandy L. "The Incumbency Advantage." Pp. 119–41, in *Money Elections and Democracy: Reforming Congressional Campaign Finance*, edited by Margaret Latus Nugent and John R. Johannes. Boulder, Colo.: Westview, 1990.

Malbin, Michael J., and Thomas L. Gais. *The Day after Reform, Sobering Campaign Finance Lessons from the American States*. Albany, N.Y.: Rockefeller Institute Press, 1998.

McEneny, Rachel, McEneny campaign manager. Telephone interview by J. Cherie Strachan. Tape recording, Albany, N.Y., April 1998.

McGerr, Michael. *The Decline of Popular Politics: The American North, 1865–1928*. New York: Oxford Press, 1986.

Medvic, Stephen. "Professionalization in Congressional Campaigns." Pp. 91–109, in *Campaign Warriors: The Role of Political Consultants in Elections*, edited by James A. Nelson and Candice J. Nelson, Washington D.C.: Brookings Institution Press, 2000.

Morson, Berny. "School Candidates in Spending Spiral." *Rocky Mountain News* (Denver, Colo.), 18 October 1993, 17(A).

1997 Editor & Publisher Yearbook. New York: Editor & Publisher Company, 1997.

Nixon v. Shrink Missouri Government PAC, 120 S.Ct. 897 (2000).

Norton, Paul. "Liberals Win School Race." *Capitol Times* (Madison, Wis.), 2 April 1997, 2(A).

Persichilli, Karen, Jennings campaign manager. Telephone interview by J. Cherie Strachan. Tape recording, May 1998.

Putnam, Robert D. *Making Democracy Work: Civic Traditions in Modern Italy.* Princeton, N.J. Princeton University Press, 1987.

Ragatz, Tom, Madison School Board candidate. Telephone interview with J. Cherie Strachan. Tape recording, September 2001.

Rich, Jonathan M. "Campaign Finance Legislation: Equality and Freedom." *Columbia Journal of Law and Social Problems* 20, no. 4 (1986): 409–36.

Rogers, Everett M. *Diffusion of Innovations,* 3rd ed. New York: Free Press, 1983.

Russell v. Burris, 146 F.3d 563 (1998).

Sabato, Larry. *The Rise of Political Consultants.* New York: Basic, 1981.

"Sadly, Big Money Politics Comes to Town." *Capitol Times* (Madison, Wis.), 13 March 1997, 1(C).

Salamore, Barbara G., and Stephen A. Salamore. *Candidates, Parties and Campaigns: Electoral Politics in America,* 2nd ed. Washington, D.C.: CQ Press, 1989.

Sarasota Herald Tribune, October 15 1999–4 February 2000.

Schaffner, Brian F. , Matthew J. Streb, and Gerald C. Wright. "A Rule That Works: The Nonpartisan Ballot in State and Local Elections." Paper presented at the Midwest Political Science Association Meeting, Chicago, April 1999.

Schlesinger, Joseph. "The New American Political Party." *American Political Science Review* 79, no. 4 (December 1985): 1152–69.

Schrader, Dennis, Howard County executive candidate. Telephone interview by J. Cherie Strachan. Tape recording, October 2001.

Shea, Daniel M. "The Passing of Realignment and the Advent of the 'Base-Less' Party System." *American Politics Quarterly* 27, no. 1 (January 1999): 33–57.

———. *Campaign Craft: The Strategies, Tactics and Art of Political Campaign Management.* Westport, Conn.: Praeger, 1996.

Shea, Daniel M., and Stephen C. Brooks. "How to Topple an Incumbent." *Campaigns & Elections* 16, no. 6 (June 1995): 20–29.

Shrink Missouri Government PAC v. Maupin, 71 F.3d.1422, 1424 (1995).

Shrink Missouri Government PAC v. Adams, 161 F.3d 519 (1998).

Snowden, Carl. Annapolis mayoral candidate. Telephone interview by J. Cherie Strachan. Tape recording, September 2001.

Sorauf, Frank J. "Competition, Contributions and Money in 1992." Pp. 78–83, in *Campaigns and Elections American Style,* edited by James A. Thurber and Candice J. Nelson. Boulder, Colo.: Westview, 1995.

———. *Money in American Elections.* Boston: Scott, Foresman and Company, 1988.

St. Petersburg Times, 6 January 1999–10 February 2000.

Taylor, Marissa. "Southlake Candidate Raises the Bar in Financing Race." *Fort Worth Star-Telegram,* 8 April 1998, 6.

The Baltimore Sun, 29 June–5 November 1997, and 1 September–25 October 1998.

"The Cost of Campaigning." *The Bradenton Herald,* 24 October 1999, 7(B).

The Municipal Yearbook, 1996. Washington, D.C.: International City/County Management Association, 1996.

The News Tribune (Tacoma, Wash.), 3 May–19 September 2001.

"The Inauguration: We Force the Spring." *New York Times,* 21 January 1993, 15(A).

Thurber, James, A. "Introduction." Pp. 1–8, in *The Battle for Congress, Consultants, Candidates and Voters,"* edited by James A. Thurber and Candice J. Nelson. Washington, D.C.: Brookings Institution Press, 2001.

Thurber, James A., Candice J. Nelson, and David A. Dulio. "Portrait of Campaign Consultants. Pp. 10–36, in *Campaign Warriors: The Role of Political Consultants in Elections,* edited by James A. Nelson and Candice J. Nelson, Washington D.C.: Brookings Institution Press, 2000.

Times Union (Albany, N.Y.), 31 August 1997–15 March 1998, 3 April–29 October 1993, 29 August–1 October 1977, and 31 May–11 November 1973.

Tocqueville, Alexis de. *Democracy in America.* New York: Harper Perennial, 1969.

Touhey, Carl, Albany mayoral candidate. Interview by J. Cherie Strachan. Tape recording, Albany, N.Y., May 1998.

U.S. Bureau of the Census. *County and City Databook: 1994.* Washington, D.C.: U.S. Government Printing Office, 1994.

Wattenberg, Martin. *The Rise of Candidate-Centered Politics: Presidential Elections of the 1980s.* Cambridge: Harvard University Press, 1991.

Wayne, Leslie. "Political Consultants Thrive in the Cash-Rich New Politics." *New York Times,* 24 October 2000, 28(A).

Whillock, Rita Kirk. *Political Empiricism: Communication Strategies in State and Regional Elections.* New York: Praeger, 1991.

"Woulda, Shoulda, Coulda." *Metroland* (Albany, N.Y.), 18–25 September 1997, 9.

Zausner, Robert. "Campaign Spending Limit?" *Philadelphia Inquirer,* 23 October 1998, 21(A).

INDEX

ABOUT THE AUTHOR

J. Cherie Strachan is assistant professor of communication at the University of Albany in Albany, New York. Her interest in campaign practices stems from briefly working as a press secretary and field coordinator in political campaigns prior to pursuing her PhD in political science. In addition to writing about local campaign practices, she has also published works on presidential candidates' convention films and on mock election programs in American schools. Her current research projects, which explore messages in civic education efforts and in gubernatorial candidates' campaign rhetoric, continue to address the way communication patterns affect average citizens' abilities to participate in the political process.

3921